1983

Paperweights

AND OTHER GLASS CURIOSITIES

RARE FRENCH PAPERWEIGHTS

St Louis	St Louis
Baccarat	Clichy
Baccarat	St Louis

Paperweights

AND OTHER GLASS CURIOSITIES

E. M. Elville

SPRING BOOKS

First published in 1954 by Country Life Ltd
Copyright 1954 Mrs Jane Renn
This edition first published 1967 by the Hamlyn Publishing Group Ltd
Hamlyn House · The Centre · Feltham · Middlesex
Third Impression 1968

Printed in Great Britain by Fletcher & Son Ltd,
Norwich, and bound by Richard Clay (The Chaucer
Press) Ltd, Bungay, Suffolk.

Contents

List of illustrations

The paperweights illustrated in the frontispiece are—bottom left, top right and bottom right—in the Berry-Hill Collection, New York; the others from Messrs. Delomosne and Son.

Preface

The popularity of glass paperweights has increased enormously during the last few years. Recent sales in London of large and valuable collections have stimulated public interest, and, in response to demand, articles describing the manufacture and style of paperweights have appeared in many journals during the last two or three years. The need is therefore apparent for a comprehensive and up-to-date reference to the subject.

Much has been learnt from the recent sales regarding relative values, and it is the object of this book, in extending the classification of paperweights so well begun by the French writers, R. Imbert and Y. Amic, to give some idea of valuation, a subject so far unattempted in a book of this nature.

Other glass objects outside the range usually considered by writers have been included in this book, and, as the title of the book indicates, have been classed with paperweights as 'curiosities'. The word has been used in its early sense rather than its modern meaning. In the eighteenth century a 'curiosity' could mean *an article made with art and care*, and early in the nineteenth century it still could mean *an article made with careful and elaborate workmanship*.

On the subject of paperweights, I owe thanks to Mr Cecil Davis and to Mr J. Bernard Perret, who supplied many of the illustrations. Much information regarding the valuation of paperweights was gleaned from the sales and by reference to the sales catalogues of Messrs Sotheby, which also provided a wealth of other detail. I am also indebted to Sir Hugh Chance for his kind help on the subject of Nailsea Glass, and again to Mr Davis for his illustrations and help in connection with lighting glass.

Thanks are due to the National Museum, Dublin, the Science Museum, London, the Tolson Memorial Museum, Huddersfield, and the Victoria and Albert Museum; and for their permission to publish illustrations from their collections, also to the following companies and bodies: Messrs Arthur Churchill, Ltd, Messrs Delomosne & Son, Ltd, Messrs Mallett & Son, Ltd, Messrs James Powell and Sons, Ltd, and to the Editors of *The Connoisseur, Glass, Country Life* and *Country Life Annual*.

E. M. ELVILLE

9

CHAPTER ONE

The Origin and Manufacture of Paperweights

IF it had been possible to have gazed into those fascinating crystal globes, which, for want of a better name, today we term paperweights, and to have foreseen the popularity they have achieved in recent years, then without doubt our grandparents would not have banished them to the back of bookcases or disused drawers, but would have treated them with more becoming dignity. Purchased then for a few shillings, paperweights have risen in value in meteoric fashion to change hands in the sale-room at prices well over the three- and even occasionally the four-figure mark, and continue to do so.

An interesting comparison in values can be made by tracing the rise in prices over the last forty years. Way,[1] in an article on paperweights in 1920, made the following comments on price: 'The prices of paperweights since the year 1912 have gone up in leaps and bounds. Prior to that year, dated glass paperweights could be picked up for ten or twelve shillings, whereas now they have risen to four, five and six pounds, and undated weights which could be purchased for five shillings have risen to two, three and five pounds, according to beauty of design and good workmanship.'

From my own records, it is evident that the value of paperweights roughly doubled between the wars, for in 1939, a good dated Baccarat millefiori weight could be purchased from £6 to £12. At that time a good overlay weight was valued between £10 and £15.

There has been only one serious attempt to classify glass paperweights.[2] Although the classification is an excellent one, it is not complete and no effort was made to deal with rarity and relative value. In the present book, the classification goes farther, and grouping has been made on the basis of rarity which, in the main, forms the basis of value with many paperweights. The prices given in the next chapter are those which applied during the famous London sales when the large collections of the late Mrs Applewhaite-Abbott and others were sold. Although the *actual* value of paper-

[1] W. H. L. Way, *Connoisseur*, December 1920.
[2] R. Imbert and Y. Amic, *Les Presse-Papiers Français*, France, 1948.

11

weights may rise or fall according to circumstances, their *relative* value will vary very little from those given.

ORIGIN OF THE PAPERWEIGHT

Fundamentally, the idea of the glass paperweight was Venetian, but the decorative feature that ensured its ultimate popularity and value was Egyptian in origin. This was the millefiori form of design, a mosaic pattern built up from sections of multi-coloured rods or canes embedded in the thickness of the article. The name millefiori is not an ancient one; it is an Italian word meaning a thousand flowers, first used by the Venetians when they re-introduced the technique of making such patterns during the Renaissance.

Millefiori patterns had then been known for centuries. Egyptian vessels remarkable for their beauty of outline and richness and harmony of colour, with decoration of inlaid or mosaic form, still exist today; they date from the fourteenth and fifteenth centuries B.C. The making of the mosaic was ingenious; blobs of glass of different colours were placed together and heated until they became welded into a whole, but not to a point at which the colours would mix. The hot, plastic mass was then drawn into a long cane, the pattern or mosaic formed by the original colours being perfectly retained in the reduced section of the cane. The process has a modern counterpart in the production of the sticks of 'rock' which advertise with every succulent mouthful the name of the seaside town in which they are made. Sections of the mosaic canes cut either square or obliquely were then placed together, reheated, and finally moulded into the shape required.

Following the Roman conquest of Egypt in 27 B.C., the art did no more than follow the traditional lines, and by the first century A.D., the Roman technique had advanced to the stage which is today understood by millefiori. Many examples of Roman art of this nature are found in museums throughout the world.

It is true, of course, that the Venetians mastered the art of millefiori, and were the first to apply this form of decoration to paperweights. Indeed, it was Marcantonio Sabellico, the learned librarian of St Mark's and historian of Venice, who first called attention to them. In his book, written *c.* 1495,[1] Sabellico referred to the industry of Murano, the little island off Venice, devoted then, as it is now, to glass-making. 'A famous invention first proved that glass might feign the whiteness of crystal, and they began to turn the material into various colours and numberless forms — but consider to whom

---

[1] Marcantonio Sabellico, *De Situ Venetae Urbis.*

did it first occur to include in a little ball all the sorts of flowers which clothe the meadows in spring.'

Although the technique does not appear to have been exploited to any great extent in Venice, nevertheless, the credit is given to that centre for originating the modern version of the paperweight. The earliest recorded paperweight is a Venetian specimen by Pierre Bigaglia. This weight is in the shape of a two-inch cube, and is decorated with latticinio and signed and dated canes, some bearing the initials P.B. and the date 1845.

Latticinio — literally, lace glass — contained fine threads of glass, usually white, but sometimes coloured. The technique of preparing latticinio was somewhat similar to that of millefiori. Sticks of opaque-white glass were placed round the inner surface of a small cylindrical hollow mould, and the whole heated. Soft, colourless glass was then poured into the mould, and the mass withdrawn and stretched into a long cane. The enamel glass now appeared as cotton-like threads twisted throughout the cane.

Other weights by Bigaglia followed the conventional spherical style, some of which are extant. One changed hands in London in 1952, signed P.B. and dated 1845, one cane bearing the following inscription 'IX Congreso Degli Scienziata in Venezia 14'. The paperweight was composed of latticinio twists and millefiori canes.

This style of paperweight was shown at an Exhibition of Austrian Industry held at Vienna in May 1845, and was noticed by M. Peligot of the Paris Chamber of Commerce. His report stated: 'one of the principal exhibits is that of M. Pierre Bigaglia of Venice — round-shaped millefiori paperweights of highly transparent glass in which are embedded numerous small canes of all colours and forms, assembled to look like a posy of flowers'.

No time would appear to have been lost, for in the same year, 1845, a vase about six inches in height was made at one of the French factories, probably St Louis, with drawn trumpet bowl, diamond-faceted knop on the stem, and a millefiori base. The interesting feature concerning this specimen is that the date is reversed, that is, it is a mirror image of the correct date, a mistake which suggests that the technique was a new one, and not at that time completely mastered. This specimen changed hands in London in 1939. A similar St Louis specimen, but undated, is shown in Plate 5(A).

The real art and technique of producing paperweights, however, belongs without doubt to the French glass-makers, and three factories producing them a century ago are famous names today among collectors all over the world; they are Baccarat and St Louis, both in the Vosges mountains, and Clichy, Paris, where a glassworks functioned between 1840 and 1870.

There were, of course, other factories producing paperweights in France and in other countries, and occasionally a valuable weight changes hands which it is impossible to assign to any particular factory. For example, a salamander weight changed hands recently for the record sum of £1300. It showed a green and yellow reptile curled on a rockwork base, the body darkening towards the tail, which was translucent. The ground was clear glass and the dome high. A feature of the weight was its unusual size, four and a half inches. This weight was not attributed to any particular factory.

The popularity of the millefiori paperweights from Baccarat, St Louis and Clichy is well-deserved, for they excel in design, quality of colours, and especially in workmanship. The patterns are of infinite variety — it is impossible to find two specimens exactly alike — and of every conceivable tint both in transparent and opaque glass. They display, more than any others, a masterful technique in arrangement of the patterns and especially in the minute forms in the canes of animals of all descriptions. These motifs are faithful reproductions in detail and form — there is nothing crude about them in delineation. Figures of such subjects as a mountain goat or a dancing girl may appear little bigger than a pin's head even under the magnification of the convex globe in which the set-ups are embedded, yet they are exactly reproduced in all detail.

THE MAKING OF A PAPERWEIGHT

The set-up of a paperweight required much patience and preparation. The method employed in making millefiori, for example, was somewhat similar to that used by the ancient craftsmen to produce mosaic patterns, already described on page 12. The first requisite was a number of small pots of glass of different colours. A rod of iron, known as the gathering iron, was rolled over the surface of the molten glass in one of the pots, allowing a small quantity of the soft mass to adhere to the tip of the iron. The glass was then shaped into a cylinder by rolling it over a slab of polished iron called the 'marver' — molten glass behaves much like putty or dough when it is soft — and then plunged into a pot of a different colour. The soft glass adhered to the cylindrical core encasing it evenly and uniformly. The mass was again rolled over the marver to re-establish the former cylindrical shape, and the process repeated with a third colour.

In most cases, the soft mass was finally shaped into a hexagon,

star, or some such outline by being plunged into a shallow mould —
something like a small pastry mould — of that shape. A second iron
rod, or pontil, was then attached to the other end of the cylinder of
glass by a second workman; the two men next walked slowly apart,
the soft mass of glass suspended between them being stretched into
a thin cane. When the drawn cane was something less than a mille-
metre in thickness, it was dropped into a wooden trough, and
allowed to cool.

This process was repeated time and time again to form canes of
different colour combinations and shapes. In addition, canes were
prepared with the silhouettes of figure subjects; this required a
somewhat modified technique. An open iron mould had first to be
carved on the inside to the shape of the motif required. In making
the cane, the mould was heated and a mass of soft glass, usually of a
dark colour, was dropped into it. When the glass was sufficiently set
but still hot, the mould was opened, the moulded motif removed by
being attached to a pontil rod, and coated with a layer of glass of
contrasting colour, usually opaque white. This was then reheated
and stretched, as in the case of the floret motif, into a long cane.
The silhouette of the motif would retain its shape perfectly, and
would appear as a tiny dark figure against its contrasting light background.

There is a variety of subjects for these central motifs: deer, dogs,
horses, camels, elephants, demons, goats, butterflies, monkeys and
dancing figures. It is not at all uncommon to find half-a-dozen such
motifs in one paperweight, as well as myriads of tiny florets and
posies of multi-coloured blossom.

The next stage in the manufacture of the paperweight was to
arrange the canes into a design, and this was probably the most
important one. It was done, of course, when the canes were cold.
An iron mould was required for the operation; it was an open
mould, rather like a thick, flat ring, to which a handle was attached.
The ring was placed on a bed plate, and short lengths cut from canes
selected to blend for colour and design, were bundled together into
the core of the mould. Cavities left between them were filled with
canes of colourless crystal or sometimes with opaque and tinted
glass. It was not at all unusual for a hundred bundles or so to be
inserted in the mould, each bundle itself consisting of half-a-dozen
up to perhaps fifty separate canes.

Next, the mass was heated to softening point so that the canes
became welded together. It was then withdrawn from the mould by
a pontil rod, and coated with successive layers by being plunged into

a pot of crystal glass, until it had been built up to its correct size. The final process was to anneal the paperweight by cooling it slowly in a kiln, in order to remove stresses in the nature of the material that would cause it to crack or fracture.

It has already been stated that the design and patterns of paperweights were such that it is impossible to find two specimens alike. Nevertheless, paperweights fall into certain groups based on their similarity. For example, the millefiori have already been subdivided into Baccarat, St Louis and Clichy, and each group may be further subdivided depending on its style of decoration, patterns, and finish. In addition, there are other styles of paperweights in which representations of flowers, fruit, and insects are embedded, and which are highly prized by connoisseurs. A different technique was used for the making of such paperweights. The motif was first made of enamel glass of delicate colouring either by moulding or by hand-working, and then embedded while hot in a globe of clear crystal glass by the usual gathering process.

Also highly prized by connoisseurs are the overlay paperweights. Overlays were usually made with the millefiori mushroom in a crystal globe which was given a thin coating of white opaque glass and a final casing of a colour such as red, blue or green; specimens are shown in Plates 1(E) and 4(E). 'Windows' were then cut by grinding and polishing on the top and sides to expose the millefiori centre. The edges of the windows show a thin lining of the white opaque underlayer which greatly enhances the general effect.

CRYSTALLO-CERAMIE OR INCRUSTATIONS

There was another type of decoration used by both French and English factories which depended on encasing in the body of a paperweight a porcelain-like cameo of such subjects as busts of crowned heads and other famous people, sporting scenes, medallions, seals, coats-of-arms and floral designs. These objects are also known as 'sulphides' or 'incrustations'.

The process would appear to have been first employed in Bohemia about 1750 and was later developed by the French factories. A French glass-maker named Desprez was making cameos in a porcellaneous material, and enclosing them in clear glass towards the end of the eighteenth century. A specimen of his work is preserved in the Sèvres Museum. In the beginning of the nineteenth century patents were granted in France to various manufacturers, and a brisk sale of paperweights of this type was conducted in Paris, notably at the well-known establishment *À l'Escalier de Cristal*.

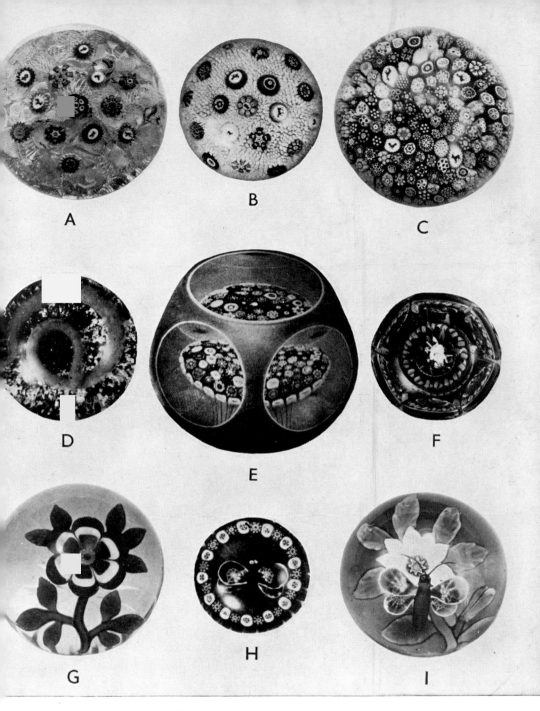

1. BACCARAT PAPERWEIGHTS

A: 'Upset Muslin', B 1848. B: 'Stardust', B 1848. C: Cluster of millefiori and animal canes, dated B 1848. D: Light green mottled snake. E: Overlay with millefiori tuft. F: Bouquet faceted weight. G: Primrose with six blue and white petals. H: Butterfly on clear glass ground. I: Butterfly with mauve body and multi-coloured wings (*All except E from Messrs Delomosne & Son.*)

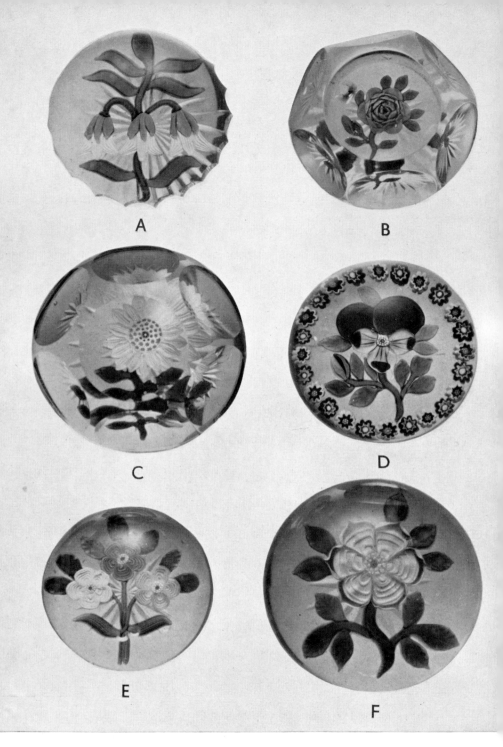

2. BACCARAT PAPERWEIGHTS

A: Bell flowers with white petals and green foliage. B: Pink rose, a rare Baccarat flower. The sides are faceted and cut with stars. C: Unusual Baccarat flower, possibly a marguerite. D: Pansy with mauve and yellow petals enclosed in a garland of green and white canes. E: Rare bouquet 'tricolore' weight with three buttercups, pink, white and pale blue with bright green foliage. F: Unusual Baccarat flower with six white petals tipped pinkish-red, and bright green foliage. (*All from Messrs Delomosne & Son.*)

Specimens of this early work are preserved at the museum at Hamburg.

Experiments were being conducted in this country at the same time, and following the granting of the French patents, Apsley Pellatt took out a patent in 1819 which was described as a process for the making of crystallo-ceramie or glass incrustation.

Apsley Pellatt, when only thirty, founded in 1821 the Falcon Glasshouse in Southwark, London, and at once devoted his energies to the development of his patent. Pellatt himself admitted that the idea was fundamentally French.[1] He formed his incrustations from china clay and a frit of potash and sand, of such proportions that the final paste had a higher fusion point than that of the glass in which it was to be embedded. The method was thus described by Pellatt:[2] 'By the improved process, ornaments of any description — and landscapes of any variety of colour, may be introduced into the glass. The substance of which they are composed is less fusible than glass and may previously be formed by either moulding or modelling, and it may be painted with enamel colours which are fixed by exposure to a melting heat. Specimens of these incrustations have been exhibited not only in decanters and wineglasses, but in lamps, girandoles, chimney ornaments, plates and smelling bottles. Busts and statues on a small scale to support lamps or clocks and masks after the antique, have been introduced with admirable effect.' Specimens of these incrustations will be discussed in Chapter Three.

In connection with this work Apsley Pellatt took out a patent in 1831 for an open-and-shut mould for making his 'glazed pottery'. The inside of the mould was carved in intaglio with the required design. The refractory paste was then pressed into it to produce a cameo cast, which was dried, fired, and when required was heated to a dull red heat. Molten glass was then poured over the cast, and the paperweight built up to the shape required by successive gatherings of molten glass.

Several French factories used incrustation as a form of decoration for paperweights, and many interesting specimens have changed hands recently. They will be considered in the next chapter under the title of the factory at which they were made.

---

[1] A. Pellatt, *Glass Manufactures*, London, 1821.
[2] A. Pellatt, *Memoir on the Origin of Glassmaking*, London, 1845, pp. 30 *et seq.*

CHAPTER TWO

French Paperweights

BACCARAT

IN the main, Baccarat weights can be divided into two main groups, namely, millefiori, which form roughly two-thirds of all Baccarat weights, and flowers, which comprise a little less than one-third. In addition, there is a small group, which in all does not amount to five per cent, with a subject, such as reptiles and butterflies; from the point of value, this is by far the most important group. Finally, there are incrustations, which represent a very small proportion of Baccarat weights.

The classification of all Baccarat weights is as follows:

Millefiori	Rare Subjects
Overlay	Butterflies
Tufts	Magnums
Grounds	Miniatures
Flowers	Incrustations

Millefiori

This would at first appear a difficult group to classify. Actually, however, there are well defined lines of demarcation which make grouping fairly easy. First, the figured and dated millefiori are all much of the same pattern. Examples are given on Plate 1 (A, B and c) — all three dated B.1848. I have found from an examination of a very large number of Baccarat weights that very approximately half the millefiori type are dated. Although Imbert and Amic[1] in their classification of Baccarat weights state that 'a few millefiori are dated', this would appear to be a bad translation from the French text.

The dates are from 1846 to 1849 inclusive, the most common being 1848 and the rarest 1849. About seven out of every ten dated Baccarat weights will bear the date 1848, one in five will be dated 1847 and one in ten, 1846. The date 1849 is exceedingly rare.[2]

The figures are usually in separate canes of red, blue or green against a white background. The order of the colours varies and

[1] R. Imbert and Y. Amic, *op. cit.*, p. 69.

[2] There is a record of a French paperweight with the date 1845, but as the 5 in the date is most indistinct, it is considered to be most probably 1848.

appears to follow no definite sequence. In many cases the weights are initialled by a tiny letter B in one of the canes. An occasional weight has some other letter, probably a workman's initial, the letters J and F being known.

An initial and date do not necessarily enhance the value of a paperweight, though the date may be a rare one. For example, two Baccarat weights marked with the rare date 1849 recently changed hands in a London sale room, one at £38 and the second at £240. The difference in value was due entirely to the rarity of the design. The first had the usual tightly packed and brightly coloured florets, and animal silhouette canes; the other had a rare chequer design of turquoise rods on a latticinio gauze ground, each square containing a different floret or silhouette cane.

Much the same applies to the commoner dates. As an example, in the sale-room recently two adjacent lots were Baccarat weights both dated 1848; one sold at £45 and the other £270, the difference being due entirely to the rarity of the set-up. The first had the usual evenly spaced silhouette and floral canes, the other the same florets but in a red 'carpet' ground comprised of tightly packed miniature canes. The so-called carpet ground in millefiori (described on page 20) is rare, and rarity in the design of a ground is a most important characteristic in deciding the value of a paperweight.

It has already been stated that half the millefiori type are signed and dated, and therefore easily identified; the remainder consists mainly of plain millefiori, but recognizable by certain characteristic markings in the canes. These may be in the form of well defined arrows which are set in a circular cluster of white triangular rods. The apexes of the rods and the points of the arrows are all directed to the centre of the cluster. Occasionally the white rods have an outer lining of blue, green or red. The arrows are usually green or blue.

A star-shaped rod is another feature in Baccarat millefiori. These are usually in one colour marked with a differently coloured dot, or alternatively a cylindrical cane with a hollow star-shaped centre.

Few of the ordinary Baccarat millefiori weights are of any great value. During the London sales in 1951–3, when a large number of these weights changed hands, more than eight out of every ten realized less than £50 each.

Overlays

A description of overlay weights has already been given on page 16. A Baccarat specimen is shown in Plate 1(E).

Baccarat overlay weights are uncommon, amounting to less than two per cent of all Baccarat weights. They are all fairly similar in design, the mushroom or tuft of millefiori being enclosed in a faceted casing of a colour over white. The usual overlay colour is turquoise, but bright blue overlays are known. A few have traces of the original gilt scroll decoration on the overlay colour. The tuft is composed of the usual coloured florets in red, white, blue and other colours, some having small arrows, typical of Baccarat millefiori, set in canes pointing towards the centre of the tuft. The arrows may be in one colour or two alternate colours. There are five windows cut in the side, with a larger one at the top, but six-sided specimens are known. Nearly all have the star-cut base. The weights vary between two and seven-eighths inches to three and one-eighth inches.

Prices vary according to rarity of design; in the 1951–3 sales Baccarat overlays changed hands from £105 to £290.

Tuft Weights

Some of the tuft weights — not of the overlay type — have the millefiori mushroom encircled by a rope of entwined coloured and white spirals. There is a rope usually of blue in the ring, but scarlet ones are very occasionally met with. These weights have a some-what higher value than the usual millefiori weights and have fetched prices up to £115.

Grounds

Reference has already been made to the importance of the carpet ground, examples having been given on page 19 of a rare chequer carpet ground composed of turquoise rods on a latticinio ground, and of a red carpet ground of tightly packed miniature canes. The carpet ground in both cases considerably enhanced the value of the weight. The term carpet was first used in the *Catalogue des Collections du Conservatoire des Arts et Metiers*, Paris, of 1855, to describe a tightly packed cushion of stars made from millefiori canes of various colours. A highly valued St Louis specimen is shown on Plate 3(G).

In addition to the examples already given, the carpet grounds most highly prized by connoisseurs are the tightly packed miniature canes in combinations of colours, such as blue and white and pink and white, or in single colours such as turquoise, red, or green. There are the usual florets and silhouettes, and in some cases the weights are initialled and dated, but as already pointed out, such features make no difference to the value, which is based solely on the rarity of the carpet design.

Rare carpet grounds represent about three per cent of all Baccarat weights, prices in the 1951–3 sales varying between £105 and £270.

Flower Weights

The flower weights are an interesting group, and those with natural colouring and excellent craftsmanship are collectors' favourites. Some have individual flowers, but others with garlands and posies of mixed blooms are classed as 'bouquets'.

The most common individual flowers are primroses, pansies and clematis, which, in equal proportions, comprise together roughly two-thirds of the flower weights. Then come buttercups, camomiles, tulip-buds, and undefined flowers which account for nearly one-third. The more uncommon varieties are narcissus, anemones, bell-flowers, daffodils and roses, but the fact that they are scarce does not necessarily enhance their value. Indeed, individual flower weights, with few exceptions, are comparable in price with the commoner millefiori weights.

Primroses: The more usual style is a blue and white flower, which may be composed of white petals with a dark blue lining or of blue and white stripes (Plate 1, G). Occasionally there is a blue bud. An uncommon colour is crimson, sometimes with smaller, white-edged crimson petals inside larger plain crimson ones.

In some cases the flower, with its green foliage, has an outer ring of florets, such as alternate red and white either on a clear glass ground or on latticinio. There are five or six petals to the flower, more commonly six.

Pansies: The commoner style is a flower with five petals, which are in two colours, yellow or golden colour with amethyst, crimson or purple. The specimen shown in Plate 2(D) has a yellow and mauve flower encased in a garland of green and white canes. Most specimens have one bud and emerald green foliage.

Imbert and Amic[1] mention that most probably the earliest pansy model had the three petals of the lower part of the flower of transparent blue crystal with a ribbed outside coating and veins of white enamel. This style must be rare, for I have so far not encountered one.

Clematis: This motif may be of a five- or six-petalled flower of a single or double type. The colours are varied, consisting of white, blue and white, bright red, red and black, and reddish pink, with centres of dark red or pale yellow. There is usually foliage in

[1] R. Imbert and Y. Amic, *op. cit.*, p. 73.

emerald green, yellowish green, or white and green, some specimens having a single bud.

Many specimens have a circle of florets of alternate red and white, blue and white, or green and white canes set in clear glass or in a muslin ground.

Rarer specimens of clematis have blue and white and blue-spotted white petals with red, or red and white, centres. These rare weights changed hands at the £70 mark, but the more common varieties are valued at half this sum.

Buttercups: Roughly ten per cent of the Baccarat flower weights are of the buttercup type, consisting of white petals with blue stripes, or turquoise blue and white, or red and white. An occasional specimen has double flowers with white petals set in large pink ones. All have green foliage, and every other one has a single red bud. Prices have varied recently, depending on colour and workmanship, from £24 to £115. A rare buttercup bouquet is shown in Plate 2(E).

Camomile or Pom-Pom: The flower in this case is almost invariably white — very seldom blue — made up of concentric rows of fine white petals. The centre of the flower varies somewhat, typical styles being yellow florets in various patterns, or yellow honeycombing. Some camomile weights have two buds which may be above the flower, or one on each side, usually in green, or green and white, with emerald green leaves up to six in number, with stalks. The leaves may also be white.

An occasional weight has only one bud. There may be a garland of millefiori canes surrounding the central motif, either in green and white or red and white florets.

Imbert and Amic[1] state that all the camomile weights are on a clear crystal ground. A camomile weight, however, which recently changed hands, had a white flower with blue and yellow floret centre, a single bud and four green leaves, set on a translucent pink and opaque white swirl ground.

Most camomile weights are faceted, and have a star-cut base. These weights are not rare, representing about seven per cent of all Baccarat flower weights.

Tulip Buds: Roughly three per cent of the flower weights are tulip buds, usually in pink, or pink and white fluted; an occasional blue one is found. The arrangement of the buds may be in groups of two or three, two groups appearing on each weight, joined together with emerald green stalks and foliage.

[1] R. Imbert and Y. Amic, *op. cit.*, p. 73.

Anemone: Less than two per cent of the flower weights consist of anemones. The usual flower is brilliant blue edged with white, or white with red borders. The centres are often red and white. The stems are bright emerald green, usually with some green foliage. The bases are star-cut.

Narcissus: These represent less than two per cent of all Baccarat flower weights. The petals may be white with blue spots, or pale blue, and the centres composed of florets in various colours, or in a single colour, such as violet. The flower is accompanied by a bud and yellowish or emerald green foliage. The narcissus weights are valued somewhat higher than other flower weights, prices from £60 to £80 being recorded.

Bell Flower: Bell flowers are rare, about one per cent of all Baccarat flower weights being of this type. The flowers may be blue, red or white (Plate 2, A), with one or more buds and green foliage. A weight with flowers in two colours is very rare. One that changed hands recently for £105 had two red and two white flowers, a red bud, and four leaves set in a clear ground.

Daffodil: Only one in a hundred of the flower weights is of the double daffodil type, although the fact that they are so scarce does not appear to enhance their value. The flower is usually white, but other colours, such as blue and pink, are known. The white flowers often have a blue centre. There are usually one or two buds with green foliage. They all have star-cut bases, and an occasional specimen is faceted.

Fuchsia: Baccarat weights featuring a fuchsia are very rare, representing something less than one in a hundred of all Baccarat flower weights. The usual style is a reddish pink flower and bud, suspended from a light brown stem with numerous emerald green leaves. The ground is of clear glass. Prices are about the £50 mark.

Rose: This is probably the rarest of all Baccarat flowers. A particularly beautiful specimen is shown in Plate 2(B) of a pink rose of natural formation, and green foliage. The weight is faceted, with stars cut on the sides. Roses vary in colour from light pink to deep red. Prices approach the £100 mark.

Bouquets: Although nearly one-third of all Baccarat weights are flower weights, very few have a bouquet of flowers for a subject; certainly less than three per cent. A common style of bouquet is the so-called 'tricolore', in which a central motif, such as a buttercup or blue flax flowers, with light green foliage and stems, are flanked left and right by red and white primroses or white clematis, all on a clear glass ground. A somewhat similar 'tricolore' specimen is shown on Plate 2(E).

Another style is an upstanding spray of flowers in various colours with light green leaves with a coloured latticinio rope round the base, or a central bouquet of flowers such as clematis flanked by pansies, roses and buds with bright green foliage. A typical specimen is illustrated in Plate 1(F). This has a latticinio spiral with blue spiral and an amber flash ground. It is faceted on the top and sides.

A feature of the foliage of Baccarat bouquets is the crossed stalks. This is not noted on weights from other factories. Most bouquet weights have the basal star, and an occasional one is faceted on the top and sides. Another feature of bouquet weights is that they are somewhat larger than other weights, the size varying between three inches and three and five-eighths inches. Prices are usually over the three-figure mark, varying in the 1951–3 sales between £105 and £360.

Rare Subject Weights

The Baccarat factory produced a small number of weights with subjects such as caterpillars, snakes, ducks and butterflies, and these are among the most valued of all Baccarat weights.

A caterpillar weight changed hands in London in 1952 for £1200.

These weights are exceedingly rare, only two or three specimens being known. The specimen referred to showed four mushroom-coloured caterpillars of varying sizes on a green leaf with a portion of it already eaten. The ground is of pale blue with a radiating network of latticinio canes.

Weights featuring a snake are not so rare, probably comprising about one per cent of all Baccarat weights. The snake is usually in bright colours such as blue, and pink or green, with reddish brown or darker green markings, or red with black markings, and lies coiled on a ground which may consist of muslin canes or of rockwork in various colours such as green and silver or those suggesting quartz. A typical specimen is shown on Plate 1(D), with a light green mottled snake on a green, yellow and white rocky ground. Snake weights are usually slightly over three inches in size. Prices varied in the sales of 1951–3 from £95 to £280.

A duck weight occasionally comes to light. One which changed hands recently for £440 consisted of three ducks swimming in a clear pool with a green moss-like bottom. It was cut with facets on the sides and top, and had the basal star.

Baccarat did not make a feature of fruit weights. Nevertheless, an occasional strawberry weight is met with which shows characteristics of Baccarat. One changing hands recently had two pink and two green strawberries with dark green foliage and stem. Other specimens show two red strawberries with a single green one. The fruit has coloured dots for the seed — bluish dots for the red berries, and red dots on the green fruit. Baccarat strawberry weights are rare; prices vary between £70 and £80.

Butterflies

Four per cent of all Baccarat weights feature a butterfly. They can be divided into two main classes; a butterfly alone, or with a single flower.

In both cases the butterfly has a body of a bluish tint, such as deep lilac, translucent amethyst, violet, purple or mauve, usually with a black head and antennae. Blue antennae are known. The wings are multi-coloured, usually described as marbled, the motif being set in garlands of alternate millefiori canes in red and white, or blue and white, and in some rare cases in alternate florets of red and white, and green and white, such as that shown in Plate 1(H). This has a clear glass base and a garland of red, white and blue florets. Occasionally a specimen has a pink garland of millefiori florets.

The individual flower in butterfly weights is almost invariably white, of the clematis or daffodil type, with green foliage. The motifs are so arranged that the flower occupies a central position with the butterfly below, its head and antennae falling across the flower. The dark colour of the wings, body and antennae of the insect contrast well against the light background of the flower. The green leaves are placed above the flower to complete a symmetrical balance. A typical specimen is that in Plate 1(I). The butterfly has a mauve body and multi-coloured wings and is hovering over a white flower and spray of green leaves and bud.

The ground of most Baccarat butterfly weights is of clear glass, but latticinio grounds are known. Prices vary considerably, depending on design and workmanship. Butterfly weights with a flower fetch from £60 to £290, and the individual butterfly type from £40 to £145. Imbert and Amic[1] point out the poor quality of some of the individual butterfly weights, and suggest that they may have been manufactured up to a late period. It is, of course, also well known that butterfly weights are a popular subject for reproduction. An example of a modern butterfly weight is shown in Plate 5(H).

[1] R. Imbert and Y. Amic, *op. cit.*, p. 75.

Magnums

As the name implies, magnums refer to extra large paperweights. They are all about four inches in width, and of the millefiori type. Most specimens are dated 1848, and occasionally 1847. The canes are in silhouette, geometrical and floral design, one rare specimen being known with a silhouette of a dancing man with uplifted hands.

The bases are cut with the star, raised diamonds or occasionally with strawberry diamonds. These large specimens are valued more highly than corresponding weights of the normal three-inch size, prices varying between £50 and £170. Only one Baccarat weight in a hundred is of the magnum size.

Miniatures

Millefiori: About five per cent of millefiori weights are of miniature size, varying between one and three-quarter inches to two inches in width. They are replicas of the normal three-inch mille-fiori weights with dated, animal silhouette and floret canes. The usual dates are 1847 and 1848, and most have the star-cut base. They are low in price.

Flower: About ten per cent of the Baccarat flower weights are of miniature size, varying between one- and five-eighths inches to two inches in width. Most are of the white double-clematis type with green leaves and foliage, some with a garland of alternate coloured and white floret canes. Other flowers are anemone, primrose and a six-petalled flower. They are low in price.

Incrustations

A favourite subject of Baccarat incrustations was busts or heads of famous people. Weights with cameos of Queen Victoria, the Tsar Nicholas I and Pope Pius IX are quite common.

Those of Queen Victoria show a profile of the Queen's head in dexter, usually with concentric rings of millefiori florets in white, green and red, white and green, and red, white and blue canes. The ground is of clear glass. Paperweights of this description almost invariably change hands over the £50 mark.

A standing figure of Joan of Arc within oak and laurel wreaths is also a favourite subject. These weights may have a ruby ground, and are faceted. Prices are not high.

A sporting scene with a dog as the central subject, a man with a gun, and trees in the background is another example of the commoner Baccarat incrustations. The field in the scene is in leaf-green. The sides are cut in triangular facets. These weights at three and a half inches in width are somewhat larger than usual. Prices are between £30 and £40.

Mythological figures were sometimes chosen as subjects. An upstanding bust of Aesculapius, the god of medicine, encircled by a latticinio rope with a blue ribbon, is an example of this group.

ST LOUIS

St Louis had a somewhat wider range of subjects than Baccarat. The latter factory, for example, concentrated two-thirds of its output on millefiori; St Louis, on the other hand, not only employed millefiori less extensively, but combined it in floret form with green foliage in weights with bouquet motifs. St Louis also devoted a considerable proportion of its output to flower weights, fruit, vegetables and reptiles.

A classification of St Louis weights is as follows:

Millefiori Tufts (Mushrooms)	Flowers
Millefiori Clusters	Fruit and Vegetables
Overlays	Crown Weights
Grounds	Snakes
Pedestals	Magnums and Miniatures
Millefiori floret Bouquets	

There are many distinguishing characteristics of St Louis weights. The colours are more delicate, and in some specimens pale by comparison with either Baccarat or Clichy. Characteristic colours were gentian blue, bright yellow, red, pale and bright green, and pink. Soft combinations were often featured in a specimen, such as pink, pale blue, white and yellow flowers or florets.

The proportion of signed and dated St Louis weights is much smaller than in the case of Baccarat. The usual dates are 1847 and 1848, the proportion being about one dated 1847 to every twenty dated 1848. Both red and blue are used in the figures. An occasional specimen is found with the letter SL and no date, and a few others have a date and no initial, but it is more usual for the initials SL to accompany a date (Plate 3, E).

According to Imbert and Amic[1] there is a specimen in the factory museum at Baccarat dated 1845 and initialled SL, the blue letters and figures being grouped two by two on three white canes set in a triangle.

The millefiori group, comprising millefiori alone, constitutes about twenty-five per cent of all St Louis weights. There are several styles of millefiori weights, such as the usual domed or tufted vari-

[1] R. Imbert and Y. Amic, *op. cit.*, p. 78.

ety or in the so-called scrambled or pell-mell (*macédoine*) formation, Plate 3(H). It may be argued, of course, that the millefiori floret bouquet weights belong to the millefiori group. However, by virtue of the fact that they are in imaginative floral design, and are accompanied by green foliage, they have been identified with flower weights rather than with millefiori.

Nevertheless, it will be seen from the classification that, in some form or other, millefiori weights were a staple output of the St Louis craftsmen. The canes are much the same as those of Baccarat, consisting of the usual hollow forms in various colours, usually four.

The dominating colours are blue, green and white, with a fourth colour of pink, yellow or red, mostly pink.

Millefiori Tufts (Mushrooms)

This group forms roughly half the millefiori weights, and is popular with collectors. The general pattern is a bundle of multi-coloured canes which spread out from the base in the shape of a mushroom, hence the alternative description. There is invariably a white latticinio ribbon in spiral form round the foot of the tuft, with a blue or pink ribbon encircling it. A blue ribbon is the more common colour; rare colours are salmon-pink and coral-red. (Baccarat tufts have encircling ropes.)

In most specimens the tuft is composed of florets of blue, green and white canes, usually with a fourth colour of pink, red, and occasionally yellow. They are arranged in a regular pattern of four or five concentric rings. About one in three of the tuft weights is signed and dated, the more common date being SL 1848, but this feature in no way enhances the value of a specimen. A typical St Louis mushroom weight following this description is shown in Plate 3(E). It is initialled and dated, SL 1848. Prices vary round the £60 mark.

Other tuft weights have a cluster of multi-coloured canes arranged irregularly, with a white latticinio ribbon and blue encircling spiral. Prices of such weights are somewhat higher. Rarer formations have the tuft in a basket of pink or lime yellow, red and white hollow canes. Prices of these weights vary between £185 and £240.

Most tuft weights have a star-cut base, and an occasional weight is cut with printies — circular facets — round the sides.

Millefiori Clusters

The millefiori cluster weights have the usual cushion or dome of florets instead of a tuft or sheath, and much the same plan of the arrangement of the canes is followed. In addition to the hollow canes, however, there are stars and arrows, the latter perhaps not so well defined as in the case of Baccarat.

Some St Louis millefiori canes are figured, silhouettes of animals, such as a camel, dog, fox, horse and birds, as well as dancing figures, being known. The dancing figures are popular motifs, a dancing girl and dancing demons being particularly characteristic of St Louis.

A silhouette cane often forms the central motif of a cluster weight, and millefiori canes are arranged in regular formation round it in five or six concentric circles. Colours are much the same as in the tuft weights. Prices vary considerably — £135 is the highest recorded — but are not at all influenced by the figures or by the initials and dates.

Overlays

St Louis overlay weights are highly prized by connoisseurs. The general pattern is much the same in all the overlays, the central motif being usually a bouquet of flowers with green leaves. The flowers are mostly of imaginative design with floret canes in the various colours popular with St Louis, such as blue, yellow, red and white. There is often a central bloom, such as a many-petalled white flower, or one with deep blue petals and yellow stamens.

The usual overlay colours are deep blue, apple-green or pink, with white opaque linings, or the colour may be opaque white alone. All St Louis overlays have a further casing of clear glass.

There is a further group of overlays in which the motif is composed of a bouquet of millefiori florets as described on page 30. The florets are accompanied by bright green leaves.

The windows are cut in the same style as the Baccarat weights, six windows being cut in the sides with a larger facet on the top. All specimens have a star-cut base.

The most famous of all St Louis overlays changed hands in 1957 for the record sum of £2700. The weight is encased in yellow, a colour hitherto unrecorded in overlay weights. It has a central bouquet of blue, yellow, red and white flowers and floret canes with long green leaves. The overlay was cut with six windows at the sides and another larger on the top.

Apple-green overlays are also highly prized. One which changed hands at £900 recently shows the usual coloured flowers, with green leaves, encased in apple-green lined with white. There were three windows, one on the top and two on the sides, one of which was engraved with a fox and hound.

Grounds

The importance of grounds on which the motifs are arranged has already been emphasized on page 19 in connection with Baccarat weights, and prices of St Louis weights with special grounds are as high as those of Baccarat. Grounds are of close-corrugated millefiori canes of red, pale green, pink, blue, white jasper and amber with blue. A typical specimen is shown on Plate 3(G), which has a carpet ground composed of terracotta canes with blue and white centres, set with five animal and figure canes surrounded by pale green canes; there is also a central ring of green canes.

An ordinary millefiori weight with concentric rings of multi-coloured canes centred on a silhouette cane with a dancing figure may have its value, say £50, doubled or even trebled when the motifs are displayed against a carpet ground of pale green open canes. Prices vary from £50 to £245, depending on the type of ground.

Pedestal Weights

An occasional St Louis millefiori weight is provided with a pedestal foot, which is finished in opaque white trellis latticinio. They are uncommon and fetch high prices.

Millefiori Floret Bouquets

Flowers formed over one-third of the output of St Louis paper-weights. They can be divided into two fairly equal groups: millefiori floret bouquets with green leaves, which will now be discussed, and true flowers, which will be considered in the next section.

Millefiori floret bouquets are composed of clusters of four, five and six canes of blue, yellow and white, with either pink or red — more usually pink — as a fourth colour. A six-pointed star is a popular motif for the florets, which can be blue or lined in red.

There is in most cases the same number of green leaves as of florets. The leaves are placed fan-wise behind the cluster of florets, in some cases with green stalks showing below. An occasional weight is found with pink and white florets only, with a spray of green leaves.

About half the floret weights have a garland, composed of mille-fiori canes encircling the central motif, which may be blue and pink, blue and red, pink and white or blue and white. Some weights have a white latticinio ring round the base, which may have a blue spiral.

A favourite ground is the amber flash, but as many will be found with a clear glass ground. An occasional floret weight has a latticinio ground.

It is noted that a fair proportion of the St Louis flower weights are faceted or cut with printies. Imbert and Amic[1] point out that, according to records of the Company in Paris marketing the paperweights of both St Louis and Baccarat (there was a working arrangement between the two factories), it was suggested that the bouquet weights should be cut with printies, as the motif, if set high enough, would be reflected through the printies. Many are also cut in rectangular facets or flat diamonds. A favourite decoration on the base of the bouquet weights is in strawberry diamonds or hobnail cutting.

True Flowers

True flowers constitute an equal group with millefiori floret bouquets and consist of the dahlia, clematis, camomile, fuchsia, rare flowers such as the primrose, convolvulus and jasmine, and those of imaginative design.

Dahlia: This flower is the commonest of the second group, amounting to about one-third of the true blossoms. There are usually four or five rows of petals in various shades, such as blue, bluish-purple, pink, mauve or, in some rare examples, of dark and light pink, or pink and white, and still more rarely, yellow with black markings. The centres are usually yellow, or occasionally blue, in the form of a dot or a millefiori cane, and the flower itself is backed by three, four or five — usually five — green leaves. Most specimens have a clear glass ground with basal star. The specimen shown in Plate 3(F) is characteristic of St Louis dahlia weights. It has five rows of pink petals with five small green leaves round the edge.

Dahlia weights are sought after by collectors, and usually change hands between £40 and £80. Occasional specimens, depending on colour combination and workmanship, have fetched higher prices, up to £175.

Clematis: These flowers do not occur so frequently as the dahlia, about one in six of the St Louis flower type being a clematis. The flowers are usually double, with gentian blue or pink petals and yellow centres, or occasionally with a white millefiori floret. The flower is backed by emerald-green leaves, sometimes serrated, with a stem showing below. Latticinio grounds are the most usual type, but jaspered grounds, in such colours as pink and white, are known.

[1] R. Imbert and Y. Amic, *op. cit.*, p. 77.

As in the case of the dahlia, the price of St Louis clematis varies considerably, £30 up to £115 being recorded, depending on the characteristics of colouring and finish.

Camomile: The camomile occurs less frequently than the clematis. The flower consists of closely packed petals either in pink or white, with yellow floret centre. The petals may be either single, multiple, or composed of feathers. There is usually a single bud, green leaves — invariably four — and a stalk.

The grounds vary considerably. There are cushions in swirl design in white, pink and white, or tomato red, and an occasional latticinio.

Prices are from £30 to £90, varying according to rarity and quality.

Fuchsia: Only one true St Louis flower in ten is a fuchsia. The flower is red and blue, or crimson and blue, on a slender light brown, pink or orange stem, with one or two buds. Emerald green leaves complete a colourful set-up. The ground is usually a regular, white latticinio spiral or trellis formation. Sizes vary from two and a quarter to three and a quarter inches. Prices are not high, specimens in the 1952–3 sales varying between £26 and £66.

Primrose: This is a rare flower, usually blue with five petals and a golden centre. There are the usual light green leaves, the whole being on a white latticinio regular trellis ground. Prices are about the £75 mark.

Convolvulus: In the few known specimens, the flower is pale pink with white inner petals on an emerald green stem and leaves. The ground is white latticinio in regular trellis formation. These weights are rare, one changing hands in London in 1952 for £170.

Jasmine: This flower is somewhat similar to the Baccarat double daffodil described on page 23, and is as rare. It is usually white, with ten petals and a yellow centre (Baccarat have a blue). There are the usual bright green leaves. A specimen changing hands recently in London had a blue and white jaspered cushion ground. In spite of its rarity, it fetched only £26.

Imaginative Flowers: There are several St Louis flowers of imaginative design, such as pink or blue flowers with a single or double row of petals. Pink flower-sprays are also known. All specimens have the usual green leaves, the grounds being latticinio or clear glass. A rare specimen is shown on Plate 3(D) of a white flower and green leaves set on a fine-quality red and white lattice ground.

No guide can be given as to the value of these weights. Several specimens changed hands during the recent sales at prices between £25 and £195.

3. ST LOUIS PAPERWEIGHTS

A: Fruit weight featuring a lemon. B: Rare fruit weight with strawberries. C: Two pears, an apple and four red cherries set in white lattice basket. D: White flower and green leaves. E: Tuft or mushroom with millefiori cluster, dated SL 1848. F: Dahlia with pink petals. G: Millefiori with carpet ground. H: Millefiori in scrambled, or macedoine formation. I: Crown weight with ribbons of latticinio. (*All from Messrs Delomosne & Son.*)

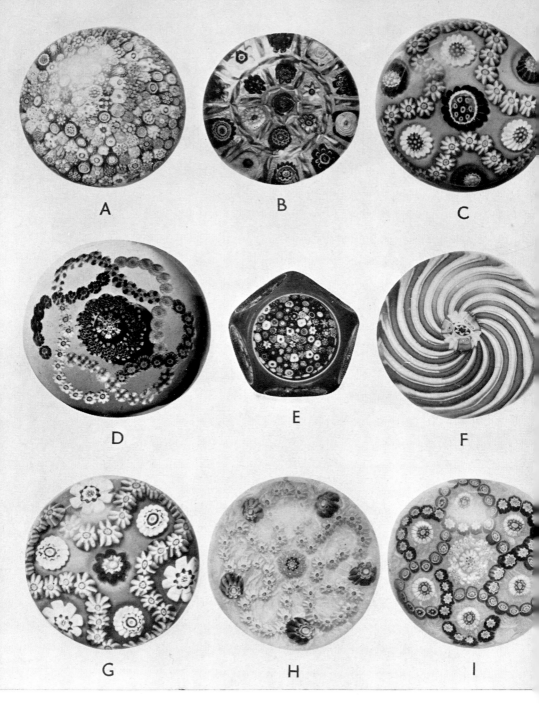

4. CLICHY PAPERWEIGHTS

A: Millefiori, signed with the letter C in a cane near the base. B: Millefiori florets on muslin ground with Clichy roses. C: Pink and white millefiori garland on opaque turquoise ground. D: Typical loop formation of millefiori florets. E: Overlay weight with large millefiori mushroom centre. F: Swirl weight in red and white. G: Garland of pink and white canes arranged in loop design. H: White muslin ground, with garland of pink florets. I: White muslin ground with entwined garland in brick-red and green.

(All from Messrs Delomosne & Son.)

5. MILLEFIORI WARE AND PAPERWEIGHTS

A: St Louis vase, cut in diamond pattern, with millefiori base. B: St Louis wafer stand
with millefiori base. C: Clichy bottle and stopper with millefiori decoration. D: Stourbridge millefiori weight. E: Stourbridge ink-well and stopper in millefiori. F: Bottle-
green paperweight. G: Flower weight with blue convolvuluses. H: Modern Scottish
butterfly weight. I: Coronation weight with Royal Cipher, E II R. (*A, B, C, E: Mr
Cecil Davis: I: Messrs James Powell & Sons Ltd.*)

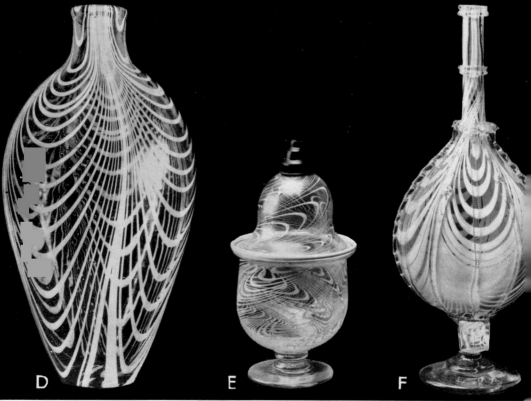

6. NAILSEA GLASS

A: Jug with flecked decorations in white and coloured enamel. B: Jug with broad encircling bands in white enamel. C: Jug in smoky green glass with white opal rim. D: Gimmal flask with white enamel festoons. E: Cup and cover with latticinio decoration. F: Bellows flask in typical 'Nailsea' style. (*B, C: Sir Hugh Chance; E, F: Messrs Delomosne & Son.*)

Fruit and Vegetables

About one in ten of all St Louis weights has a fruit motif. The fruit weights conform to a regular pattern: a bunch of fruit, such as pears, cherries, apples, etc., flanked with green leaves — usually six — resting in a white latticinio basket. A specimen illustrating this general pattern is shown in Plate 3(c); it has two pears, an apple and four red cherries with green leaves on an opaque white lattice basket.

Most fruit weights have two or three pears with three cherries, but some have only one pear and others have four cherries. Five cherries are known. The pears may be green, yellow or red, and the cherries are invariably red.

Other fruit is sometimes found in combination with pears and cherries, such as apples, plums and, rarely, an orange or a lemon (Plate 3, A). The apples are most valued when they are of pink and yellow stripes. Plums are coloured bright blue.

A rare St Louis fruit weight is one featuring strawberries. One is shown in Plate 3(B), consisting of strawberries and a white flower and green leaves on a white lattice ground.

A rare fruit weight composed of five cherries, three plums and three pears, an unusual combination of fruit, recently changed hands for £175, but the more usual varieties rarely reach the £50 mark.

Although only three per cent of all St Louis weights have vegetables as a motif, they are not highly prized specimens. The normal pattern is five, six or seven turnips set in a white latticinio basket with their points turned inwards. The colours are light purple, mauve, white and yellow. Some specimens are in red and white and are claimed to be radishes. There are usually short green stalks. Prices vary from £18 to £84.

Crown Weights

Crown weights represent about eight per cent of all St Louis weights. They are hollow blown and were used as bases for ornaments and door-knobs, as well as paperweights. The decoration is in the form of twisted ribbons of opaque white latticinio and twisted ribbon in various combinations of colours. The ribbons follow the spherical shape of the weight from the base to the top where they converge upon a millefiori cluster. A typical specimen is shown in Plate 3(I).

In most specimens, the coloured ribbons alternate with the opaque white twists. The colours are crimson and green, blue and yellow, yellow with green specks, pink and green, red, white and blue, the central millefiori cluster being lime-green, blue and white, green, and green, red and blue. These specimens vary in price from £23 to £85.

A rare specimen which recently changed hands for £130 had white-edged spirals of yellow and green aventurine glass, radiating from a blue, pink and white central cluster.

Snakes

St Louis made some excellent snake weights. The reptile lies coiled on a white latticinio gauze ground. The usual colours are pink with green markings, but a specimen is known of pale green colour with darker green markings. This reptile has red eyes. Prices are high, varying from £125 to £330.

Magnums and Miniatures

As in the case of Baccarat, a magnum St Louis is rare. They are about the same size as the Baccarat magnums, i.e., four inches in width, and are composed of concentric rows of millefiori florets in characteristic colours. Only one dated magnum weight is recorded. Prices vary between £110 and £200.

Miniature weights are not so frequent as in the case of Baccarat. They are replicas of the larger millefiori in both style and colouring. The size varies between one and a half inches and two inches. A miniature crown weight occasionally comes to light. Prices are low.

CLICHY

Less is known about the Clichy factory than those of either Baccarat or St Louis, and few records exist from which to build up authentic information. Fortunately, there are a few signed specimens which make the style of the factory recognizable. There are no dated Clichy weights, however, but it is known that paperweights were made there from about 1849. There is a variety of initials: the letters CL and ICHY in separate canes, CHY, the single letter C (Plate 4, A), or CLICHY in full, usually in blue on an opaque white background.

Clichy weights can be divided into the following groups:

Millefiori	Swirls
Overlays	Miniatures
Bouquets	Incrustations
Grounds	

Millefiori

The factory specialized in millefiori and conformed more to a standard pattern than other factories; millefiori, indeed, constitute the largest group in Clichy weights, no less than eight out of every ten being of this type. Because of this, they are the least valued of the Clichy weights.

Probably the most distinguishing feature in the millefiori weights is the so-called Clichy rose. It is made up of tightly packed leaflets either in pink or white. In the pink variety, which is the predominant colour, the outer row of leaflets alternate in green and white. Some weights have both pink and white roses. About three in ten of all Clichy millefiori weights have the Clichy rose, and one containing it can definitely be ascribed to Clichy, although the rose makes little difference to the value. The specimen in Plate 4(A) has a white rose, and that shown in Plate 4(B) has two white roses and one central pink one.

The colours used in these millefiori are of every tint in the spectrum — purple, blue, green, yellow, pink, red in various shades — with a tendency for combinations of dark colours. The colours are brighter and more brilliant than those of either Baccarat or St Louis.

Most millefiori weights are made up of multi-coloured canes whose sections give a floret design. Other motifs are star-shaped, usually in one colour with a tiny centre in another colour, or in canes with the so-called pastry-mould outline (Plate 4, C). In most cases the motifs form a design of some sort, such as clusters encircling some central motif, concentric circles of florets, loop designs (Plate 4, C, D, G, H and I), radiating panels, clusters of florets separated by latticinio spirals, horseshoe and many other attractive designs. In some specimens, however, the canes are assembled in no particular order, and are in 'scrambled' or 'pell mell' designs.

An occasional weight has the millefiori canes in mushroom form, as in the overlays, and, similar to the overlays, such weights are faceted usually with a star-cut base. Prices run somewhat higher than in the case of the ordinary millefiori.

About ten per cent of all Clichy millefiori weights are faceted, usually with five or six apertures cut in the sides with a larger one on the top, and the basal star. In many cases the facets alternate with vertical flutes. Cutting alone, however, does not enhance the value of a Clichy weight; there must be some other distinguishing feature, such as a rare ground or mushroom centre, before the value begins to soar.

Overlays

The most sought-after Clichy weights are the overlays, which comprise less than two per cent of all types of Clichy weights. Several beautiful specimens changed hands in the famous London sales in 1951–3 at prices varying between £125 and £400.

Most Clichy overlays have a rich turquoise casing, but a brilliant deep pink is also known; both colours have the usual white lining. The cutting consists of five apertures or windows cut in the sides with a larger one on the top, but an occasional specimen is found with six side windows. More than half the overlays have the base cut with strawberry diamonds. The size of the weights varies between two and a half and three and a quarter inches.

The Clichy overlay weight shown on Plate 4(E) has a large millefiori mushroom centre with pink and white outer canes. The overlay colour is a rich shade of turquoise blue, and is cut with a large facet on the top and five smaller ones on the sides. The base is cut with a pattern of fine diamonds.

The pattern of the mushroom sheaths of Clichy overlay weights varies considerably. Some specimens have the Clichy rose in a sheath of pastry-mould florets, while others consist of millefiori canes arranged concentrically in blue, white, green or pink in a basket of royal blue, green and white, or white alone.

Bouquets

Next to the overlays in importance are the weights with a central motif of a bunch of flowers, in some cases tied at the base with ribbon, hence the term bouquet weights. Many changed hands at the 1951–3 sales at prices between £100 and £200. Not so uncommon as the overlays, the bouquet weights form less than four per cent of all Clichy weights.

Some of the flowers in the bouquets are obvious, such as the pansy or the Clichy rose with bud; many are fanciful, but none-the-less attractive, designs. Typical is a bunch of three flowers of double clematis and dahlia type in such colours as blue, lilac, striped pink, mauve, dark violet, pale blue and white. Buds with green stalks and appropriate leaves or a thistle form part of some Clichy bouquets. The ribbon tying the bouquet at the base is usually pink, but an occasional specimen is found with a blue ribbon.

An unusual specimen which changed hands recently had a single lilac-pink flower consisting of ten petals in the centre with seven larger ones on the outside. The flower had a blue centre, and was set off by light green leaves. A feature of the specimen was its rare moss ground of dark green. An occasional bouquet specimen is found with a clear crystal ground.

Grounds

Examples have already been given[1] of how the ground in a paperweight may make all the difference to its value. Less than four per cent of all Clichy weights have unusual grounds. The rare colours are opaque yellow, apple-green, pompadour-rose, green muslin, scarlet and lilac. Grounds of rare patterns are often of the twisted gauze type — sometimes referred to as a muslin ground (Plate 4, H and I). The muslin grounds do not necessarily constitute rarities, as over ten per cent of all Clichy weights have latticinio grounds; it is only when the latticinio spirals are arranged in some unusual manner, such as in chequered design, that they are more highly valued.

Prices vary considerably, depending, of course, on the rarity of the ground, coupled with other distinguishing features. During the London sales in 1951–3, the prices ranged from £75 to £240, the average being round the three-figure mark.

Swirls

These are fairly common, constituting about ten per cent of all types of Clichy weights. The spirals are made up of a single colour alternating with white, the most common colours being green, purple, turquoise, pink, blue and lilac. The unusual ones are pale blue and rose pink. The specimen shown in Plate 4(F) has a swirl in red and white, with a turquoise and white central motif. An occasional swirl is found with three colours, such as pink, green and white, or purple, green and white.

The central motif may be a millefiori rosette, or floret of pastrymould canes, or occasionally a Clichy rose.

Prices are not high, the highest figure being £80 in the 1951–3 sales. This weight was a rare combination of pale blue and white centre with dark blue and white spirals.

Miniatures

Miniature Clichy weights occur rather more frequently than either Baccarat or St Louis, roughly about ten per cent of all Clichy weights being of this size. They are small replicas of the larger weights, two-thirds of them being of the millefiori type. A large proportion have the Clichy rose, similar in pattern and arrangement

[1] See p. 19.

to the larger weights. An occasional weight has a bouquet of roses and florets with green leaves.

Clusters of florets in characteristic colours are also employed on grounds of blue, latticinio and clear glass. Swirls occur less frequently and, again, are based on their larger counterparts in arrangement and design.

Sizes vary between one and five eighths to two and one-eighth inches in width, and as in the case of miniature weights from other factories, prices are low.

Incrustations

The Clichy incrustations followed much the same lines as those of Baccarat, but were confined to busts and portraits. Favourite subjects were Queen Victoria, Pope Pius IX, Napoleon and Frederick VII. The grounds of the Clichy incrusted weights were blue, turquoise, crimson or purple. Occasionally one with a green glass ground changes hands. For example, an incrustation of the French poet Alfred de Musset had a dark green ground.

The head of Napoleon was modelled by Bertrand Andrieu, and some specimens bear his reproduced signature, Andrieu B. This artist invariably showed Napoleon as a Roman Emperor with characteristic short hair and wearing a laurel wreath. The ground in most specimens is either deep blue or turquoise.

Prices of most Clichy incrustations vary between £20 and £30, but those of Queen Victoria and Napoleon fetch twice these amounts.

CHAPTER THREE

English Paperweights, Millefiori and Incrusted Ware

IT is not a difficult matter to trace that the English paperweight came into being soon after the exhibition at Vienna in 1845.[1] At that time the Stourbridge glass-makers, having been given their industrial freedom by the repeal of the Glass Excise Act in 1845, were experimenting with colour, and it is not unreasonable to assume that the first millefiori paperweights made in this country came from Stourbridge, and were based on French models. There is, indeed, a marked similarity between the paperweights known to have been made at Stourbridge, such as that shown in Plate 5(D) and, for example, some Clichy millefiori paperweights of the 1849 period.

According to some French writers, English factories were at that time engaging workmen from the Clichy factory for the making of paperweights. A comparison of two specimens, Stourbridge and Clichy, of the style shown on Plate 5(D), shows that there is the same make-up of the pastry-mould florets, and also in the general arrangement in concentric coloured rings. On the other hand, there are minor differences, but they in no way mask the parallel. For example, there are usually seven rings in the Clichy models, while the Stourbridge craftsmen, employing a somewhat larger weight, were in general satisfied with only five rings. There is also a much greater colour contrast in the different rings in the case of Clichy, due, of course, to the more intense colours employed. It will be re-called that the Clichy colours are always more brilliant than those of either Baccarat or St Louis. They are also much more brilliant than the colours chosen by the Stourbridge glass-makers, which are in the main of pastel tints compared with those of Clichy.

The parallel between the Stourbridge productions and those of the French factory is not only found in paperweights. Many other articles were made there, such as ink-stands, rulers, pen-rests, wafer-stands, and other writing-table requisites in the millefiori

[1] See p. 13.

39

style, which were for the most part flagrant imitations of the French models.

From records that still exist, it is known that in 1848 the selling company in Paris which acted for both the Baccarat and St Louis factories, suggested to the latter company that a good line of manufacture would be sets of writing-table ornaments, such as ink-stands, shot-glass pen-holders, cigar-holders, wafer-stands, etc., set on a millefiori base. Some of these were produced, and are still preserved in the factory museum. Examples of similar articles are shown on Plate 5(A, B and C). The St Louis vase (A) is six and a half inches in height with a millefiori base composed of concentric rows of canes in characteristic colours, and a white and coloured spiral rim. The vase itself is cut in diamond pattern. Another St Louis model is the wafer-stand shown in Plate 5(B). This is two and three-quarter inches high by three and a quarter inches in width at the rim, and has a scrambled millefiori base with figured canes; one cane has the figure of a dancing girl in short skirts and with outstretched arms, a characteristic feature of St Louis. The rim of the stand is in blue and white spiral form.

Bottles were also copied by the English factories. A typical model is the Clichy bottle and stopper shown in Plate 5(C). This specimen is five and three-quarter inches in height and is set on a millefiori base, with a blue and white spiral rim at the neck. The ground-in stopper is also in millefiori.

These and other models were used by the Stourbridge manufacturers, as well as others of their own conception. Some of the more usual ones are as follows, and will be briefly described: paperweights, inkwell and stopper, scent-bottle and stopper, door-knobs and newel-posts, linen-smoothers, drinking vessels, candlesticks, tapersticks and lamps, rulers, knife-rests and seals.

PAPERWEIGHTS

An example of these has already been noted (Plate 5, D) when it was pointed out that the Stourbridge paperweights are different from the French models in one or two features. In addition to these differences, the Stourbridge weights are larger than those of the French factories, the average size being three and a half inches, but four-inch weights are not uncommon. One rare millefiori weight is recorded with a diameter of five and a quarter inches. An occasional one is also found with a high crown. The shape, too, is somewhat different from the French, being finished in what is known as the 'pedestal' style, that is, with a beaded rim or foot at the base, a little wider in diameter than the body of the weight itself. The French weights have an elliptical section with a flattened bottom, whereas the Stourbridge weights appear semi-circular in section with a widened rim at the base.

The pattern of the Stourbridge weights is usually formed from regular concentric millefiori rings; each cane in a ring is of the same colour, but each ring differs in colour from its adjoining ones. The specimen shown in Plate 5(D) is typical of the Stourbridge set-ups. Usually there are five concentric rings with a central star; the colours in this specimen, from the outer rings to the centre, are blue, green, red, yellow and blue, in that order. There are over one hundred separate canes, each one consisting of an outer crinkled casing and inner core both in white opaque, with an interposed coloured ring. An occasional weight is faceted with a single row of printies round the sides.

Stourbridge also copied the Clichy grounds, typical ones being turquoise or yellow baskets set with coloured florets. Another style is a central, heart-shaped tartan-twist ribbon and a similar ribbon round the edge. Clusters are also occasionally met with, such as four green canes in a central cluster with an outer ring of clusters of red and white florets on an opaque white ground set in a blue and white basket.

BOTTLE-GREEN PAPERWEIGHTS AND DOOR-STOPS

Popular today are the bottle-green paperweights enclosing a representation of a plant growing from a pot. The pale green leaves and flowers are covered with a mass of tiny bubbles, which, under the action of reflected light, give the motif a silvery, gossamer-like appearance. They were made at Stourbridge and most other glass-making centres.

The bottle-green weights were easily manufactured. The only requisites were clear green glass such as was customarily used for bottle-making a century ago, and a few simple tools. A mass of glass was gathered and worked into the shape of an egg, chalk was sprinkled in the required design on the marver, and the soft glass pressed upon it. A second layer of glass was quickly gathered over the whole so that it was completely covered. The action of the hot glass on the chalk caused evolution of gas which was entrapped in the mass as a film of tiny, silvery bubbles.

The specimen shown in Plate 5(F) illustrates how a paperweight was built up in successive layers. There is a clear line of demarcation between the first gathering of glass, which carries the chalk motif, and the second gathering, which covers it. Often the flowers were built up in tiers, one growing from the centre of another, or in the form of fountains which stream up from the base, falling in sparkling cascades on all sides. Others are in the form of bubbles rising to the surface from the mysterious depths of a pool.

As green paperweights of the type described above were easy to make, and were formed from the cheapest glass, most bottle factories throughout the country produced them up to comparatively recent times. It was not until hand processes of producing bottles were finally superseded by automatic ones that their manufacture ceased. It is, therefore, extremely difficult to distinguish the early specimens from those of later manufacture; nor is it possible, as some writers claim, to decide from its colour where a bottle-green weight was made.

The bottle-green paperweights are ovoid in shape, with a flat base, and without exception have a pontil mark. The majority of specimens are between three and six inches in height.

DOOR-STOPS

Larger bottle-green weights are usually referred to as door-stops, and may be up to six pounds in weight. These larger variety are usually decorated with bubbles and plants in the manner described, but some are found decorated with bubbles alone. These bubbles were formed in all cases by denting the soft glass with a sharp tool, and gathering over it a further layer of glass to entrap a tiny pocket of air.

Much nonsense has been written as to the method used by glass-makers to introduce bubbles into paperweights. Perhaps the most amusing suggestion is that the bubbles were made by pricking the soft glass and inserting a spot of alcohol, the rapid evaporation of the spirit causing a bubble to form.

Alcohol was not used directly; glass-making is a thirsty business, and if alcohol *had* been supplied, no doubt the glass-maker would have found a more appropriate use for it.

In some cases the larger door-stops had bubbles in pyriform shape with a silvery thread at the narrow end. These bubbles were formed by denting the glass with a tool such as a large nail, to which a thin piece of wire was attached. The tool with its attachment was cooled, plunged into the glass, and sharply withdrawn. The layer of glass subsequently gathered over the indentation caused a pear-shaped bubble to form which tapered down to mere thread thickness. A number of these bubbles in a large door stop are very effective, giving the appearance of miniature balloons floating in space.

FLOWER WEIGHTS

Another style of paperweight, popular in this country about the middle of the last century is the so-called 'flower' weight. The making of these weights was similar to that used in the French factories, but the quality both in style and finish left much to be desired. The motif, such as a representation of flowers, fruit or an insect, would first be made of coloured enamel glass as near natural tints and shades as possible. Some of the motifs were moulded, but others were made entirely by hand. After completion, the motif was laid face down in a shallow mould, heated, and covered with fluid crystal glass. A 'pontil' rod was then attached to the soft glass, which was withdrawn from the mould, and covered by successive layers of glass by the gathering process until the requisite size was attained. The shape required was finally completed by manipulation of the plastic mass on the marver plate.

A typical specimen of flower paperweight is shown in Plate 5(G), with bright blue convolvuluses growing from a grass-green pot. The flowers have been given a natural touch by a bubble, representing a dew-drop nestling in the centre of each flower.

MODERN PAPERWEIGHTS

Paperweights are still made in this country today, notably at Perth, Scotland, and at Wealdstone, Middlesex. The Scottish factory has been producing paperweights of the millefiori type for a number of years. They are made by a Spanish family called Ysart, who settled in Scotland in 1915. Some of the paperweights are signed PY in one of the canes, the initials of a son, Paul. The signed specimen in Plate 5(H) features a butterfly, the red initials against a white background, appearing in one of the canes below the butterfly.

Millefiori weights have also been made for many years by a firm now at Wealdstone, formerly at Whitefriars in the City of London. Many references have appeared in print regarding the so-called Whitefriars paperweights, and those bearing the date 1848 are claimed to have been made there. This type of paperweight has the usual green, blue, pink and white florets; they are sometimes faceted. No actual factory records exist, however, of the type of paperweights made at Whitefriars at that time, although it is thought that such articles have been made there more or less continuously since the middle of the nineteenth century.

The paperweight shown in Plate 5(I) is one made at Wealdstone for the Coronation of the present Queen. It is in millefiori style similar in design to the Stourbridge weights of the nineteenth century. There are five concentric rings of red, white and blue canes, with the cipher E.II.R, 1953, as the central motif.

INKWELL AND STOPPER

Stourbridge inkwells or ink-bottles are not uncommon today. The general pattern is as shown in Plate 5(E). The millefiori base is somewhat similar in pattern and colouring to the paperweights. There are five concentric rings of pastry-mould florets in red, white and blue with a central star-shaped cluster. The ground-in stopper has a similar millefiori set-up.

The height of the specimen shown in Plate 5(E) is six and a quarter inches. This is an average height, specimens varying between five and three-quarter inches and seven inches. The usual colouring is much the same as in the paperweights: green, blue, pink, yellow and, of course, opaque white. Occasionally a set is found comprising two paperweights, and ink-bottle and stopper, all in matching colours. These form an attractive group.

SCENT-BOTTLE AND STOPPER

The scent-bottles made at Stourbridge are similar to the ink-bottles just described, and much about the same size. The stopper is usually of the mushroom type and is decorated with millefiori canes matching in colour the millefiori in the base of the bottle itself. The colours of the canes are pink, yellow and blue, or red, turquoise and white.

DOOR-KNOBS AND NEWEL-POSTS

These are much the same as the paperweights in appearance, but were made with a circular section three and three-quarter inches to four inches in diameter. The millefiori decoration is with concentric rings of florets such as red, white and blue; some specimens have red shading to white at the edges. These articles are metal-mounted for attaching to doors, to be used as handles, or for attaching to the newel or upright post at the head or foot of a flight of stairs. They are mostly found in pairs.

LINEN-SMOOTHERS

Glass linen-smoothers were made long before the Stourbridge craftsmen were making millefiori. They were made in the district certainly early in the eighteenth century, but in ordinary bottle-glass. They were known as 'slickers'. Pieces of solid glass were also used for rubbing floors to give them a glossy appearance and were referred to as 'slick stones'. The early slickers or linen-smoothers had a solid base, with an attached handle about five inches long regularly knopped to ensure a firm grip. They had the appearance of an inverted mushroom.

The Stourbridge craftsmen of the middle nineteenth century found the heavy base of the linen-smoother a convenient subject for millefiori decoration. It is most probable, however, that the millefiori linen-smoothers were not part of the recognized production of the factory, but were made by the workmen for their own use. This may account for the fact that they are comparatively rare, and that in many specimens the millefiori decoration is of scattered rather than of regular formation.

DRINKING VESSELS

Many forms of drinking vessels were made in millefiori: wine-glasses, goblets, tumblers, mugs and jugs are typical of a wide range. These articles were so designed that the requisite thickness was available to take the millefiori, and its effect was enhanced by a dome-like covering of glass acting as a lens.

Wineglasses were, therefore, made with bucket-shaped bowls or waisted bell bowls which allowed a flat base, and this part was decorated with millefiori canes arranged in concentric circles. These vessels are between two and a half and four inches in height.

An alternative design, however, is the heavier goblet with slender bowl, the millefiori in this case being used to decorate a generous foot. These vessels, which are most attractive in appearance, are found up to eight inches in height. Tumblers, on the other hand, were made squatter, and, like the wineglass, rarely exceeded four inches in height. The millefiori decoration is the familiar concentric rings of coloured canes in pink, blue, yellow and green.

The jugs are quite small affairs, and were probably intended for milk or cream. They have a loop handle, and are usually between four and five inches in height. The base is heavy and decorated with the usual millefiori florets. Red and pale green honeycomb canes or blue and yellow canes were popular colours for these articles.

CANDLESTICKS, TAPERSTICKS AND LAMPS

These articles were also made in millefiori, with heavy bases decorated in concentric circles of characteristic canes. The shafts are in many cases of conical shape, the taperstick being about five inches in height, and the candlestick up to ten inches. Some candlesticks had the ordinary columnar shafts with double millefiori bases.

Lamps for burning oil were also popular articles with the Stourbridge craftsmen. They are rather massive affairs, some up to sixteen inches in height. The oil container itself may be either plain, or decorated with cut motifs, and the stem supporting the container may be plain, or decorated with opaque white spirals, or with a barley-twist finish. The foot is invariably solid and heavily made, with millefiori in honeycomb florets arranged in concentric rings of the usual Stourbridge colours.

SEALS

After 1745, when the making of coloured glass was more practised, coloured glass seals came greatly into fashion. It was found that for cheap seals, glass had one positive advantage over stone or crystal. To engrave stone or crystal by hand was a costly business, whereas designs on glass could be obtained easily by moulding. The bottle-makers had long made their seals in this manner. Thus, moulded glass fob-seals became common after 1750, and they were made in various colours, and in imitation of stone, such as cornelian.

Towards the end of the eighteenth century when colour twists were used to decorate the stems of drinking glasses, the shaft of the seal was embellished in a similar manner, and occasional specimens are today found with a twin multiple corkscrew with dark blue entwined threads. With the introduction of millefiori into this country in the middle of the nineteenth century, however, glass seals were made with the shaft decorated with millefiori florets. They are about three inches in length, and were apparently supplied with plain ends, for an occasional unengraved seal is met with.

MISCELLANEOUS ARTICLES

There were many other articles made by the Stourbridge craftsmen decorated with millefiori: bowls, salt-cellars, wig-stands, wafer-stands, rulers and knife-rests, are typical of the wide assortment of Stourbridge millefiori. The bowls were probably intended for sugar. A usual style is an ogee bowl, about five inches in diameter, with circular millefiori base.

The knife-rests and rulers are not millefiori in the true sense of the word. They were, however, made from the actual canes used for millefiori work, and contained in their length twisted canes of characteristic colours such as red, blue, green and white opaque. The knife-rests are usually about three and a half inches in length, and the rulers between nine and ten inches, by about half an inch in thickness.

INCRUSTATIONS

Reference has been made[1] to crystallo-ceramie or incrustations. The most important manufacturer of them in this country was Apsley Pellatt, and specimens of his work occasionally change hands. At one time out of fashion, incrustations have now become collectors' pieces.

Some of the many articles made by Pellatt have already been mentioned,[2] but there were numerous other pieces of a similar nature. The most popular ones were letter-weights and scent-bottles, which would appear to have constituted almost half the output of incrusted ware at the Falcon Glassworks. Other items were candlesticks, candelabra, ice-plates, cameos, seals, knife-rests, decanters, mugs, jugs for both cream and water, wafer-stands, vases and plaques.

LETTER-WEIGHTS

These articles are of the larger variety of paperweight, usually referred to as letter-weights, and they may be found up to eight inches in diameter, but smaller ones are known from two and a half inches upwards. The larger weights are often rectangular in shape with chamfered corners, sometimes with a large knop as handle, or a pyramid-shaped finial.

On most specimens of letter-weights the base is cut with strawberry diamonds, a favourite finish on Apsley Pellatt's productions. A popular subject for the incrustation enclosed in such weights is George IV as a Roman emperor. The king is shown in profile with a laurel garland in his hair, and in some specimens he is wearing the collar of the Garter above a cape tied below the neck. Another popular subject is the Duke of Wellington, and occasional ones are found with busts of classical figures such as Cupid, Bacchus and Homer.

SCENT-BOTTLES

Scent-bottles were made in great numbers at the Pellatt establishment, and in a variety of shapes. One of the standard styles is a flat pear-shaped flask between four and five inches in height with ground-in mushroom stopper. One side of the flask has an incrustation embedded in the wall, and the other is invariably embellished

[1] See p. 16.   [2] See p 17.

with cut motifs such as strawberry diamonds or relief diamonds. The sides often show pillar fluting, either plain or with diamond cutting.

There is a wide choice of subjects for the incrusted decoration: subjects of an imaginative nature, such as Cupid riding in a cockle-shell chariot being drawn by butterflies, flowers, busts of Wellington, Shakespeare, George III, George IV, William IV, Queen Charlotte, and a full-length figure of Falstaff, are a few of the more usual ones.

CANDLESTICKS AND CANDELABRA

Candlesticks and candelabra were made by Pellatt with cameo incrustations in the stem. The candlesticks are from eight inches to a foot in length, with barrel-shaped nozzles and greasepans cut in diamond facets or flutes, and embellished with pendent drops. The base is circular, cut to match the greasepan. Popular subjects for the cameo decoration are mythological subjects such as nymphs, or portraits of George IV as a Roman emperor, and other well-known figures of the times.

The candelabra are elaborate affairs. A pair recently changing hands had two gilt metal branches with nozzles and greasepans, each branch springing from incrusted medallions, one with the head of Wellington, and the other with Nelson on a pedestal. The shaft, supported on a circular scalloped foot, was cut with pillar flutes and abstract motifs. The candelabra is seventeen inches in height.

ICE-PLATES

Ice-plates were an important feature of the productions of the Falcon Glasshouse. One is illustrated in Apsley Pellatt's book,[1] in which it is said that 'several sets . . . have been executed in varied fancy or classical subjects, also with arms and crests'.

Ice-plates by Apsley Pellatt are usually found today in pairs. They are between six and seven inches in width with a star-cut base, and rims cut with a narrow border of flutes or, alternatively, with a frosted or obscured finish on the underside. The incrustations are of cameo portraits of the Duke of Wellington, Isaac Newton, Julius Caesar and other famous figures.

[1] A. Pellatt, *Memoir on the Origin of Glassmaking*, op. cit.

7. BRISTOL GLASS

A, B, C: Cruet bottles in Bristol opaque white painted in enamel colours in a style typical of Michael Edkins. D: Dark blue decanter with characteristic pear-shaped body. E: Dark blue wine-glass cooler with gilt fret border signed 'I. Jacobs, Bristol'. F: White opaque vase painted probably by Michael Edkins in Chinese *famille-rose* style. G, I: Gold-mounted scent-bottles typical of the Bristol style. H: Patch-box in dark blue glass painted in enamel colours. (*A, B, C, F: Mr Cecil Davis; D: Mrs C. Saxton; E, G, H, I: Victoria and Albert Museum.*)

A

B

C

D

E

F

9. SCONCES AND CHANDELIERS

A and C: Glass sconces of the Irish period. B: Chandelier with shallow cutting on shaft and branches; first half of the 18th century. D: Chandelier of the Regency period with chains of pendent lustres. (*A, B, C: Mr Cecil Davis; D: Victoria and Albert Museum.*)

10. PIER-GLASS MIRRORS

A: Chippendale pier-glass carved in giltwood, designed by William Ince. B: Pier-glass of the Chippendale period. C: Carved giltwood mirror in the Chinese taste. D: An Adam gilt mirror with urn motif. (*All from Messrs Mallett & Son Ltd.*)

CHAPTER FOUR

Nailsea Glass

ONE of the most fascinating studies is of the old glass presumed to have been made at Nailsea, Somerset. For the period of eighty-five years, between 1788 and 1873, this town, seven or so miles from Bristol, added its name indelibly to the list of glass-making centres in this country, but it will always remain a controversial point as to whether its popularity is merited or not.

It is possible today to recognize the so-called Nailsea style from the several collections throughout the country, notably at Taunton and Bristol Museums, and in private collections. Some of the collections were amassed from the parish of Nailsea and the neighbouring villages. In some cases pieces have been handed down through several generations, and records have been thus carefully preserved.

From a study of such specimens, it is evident that three styles are represented: (*a*) mottled or flecked ware, Plate 6(A); (*b*) ware crudely decorated in bold white festoons, such as the examples shown in Plate 6(B and C), in smoky green bottle-glass, comprising jugs, two-handled vessels, long-neck bottles, mugs and other useful articles; and (*c*) vessels quite different from those in groups (*a*) and (*b*), more sophisticated in style, with well-formed latticinio decoration in milky-white and pale pink, on a flint or pale green glass, examples of which are shown in Plate 6(D, E and F). This group comprises articles more ornamental than functional, and includes flasks, large pipes, hats, bells, shoes and bellows. They were often decorated with ruby, blue and green glass, but other colours are known, although much rarer, such as yellow and dark red.

It is quite evident that much of the ware now accredited to Nailsea was made at Bristol and Stourbridge — that at least is plain from documentary evidence; and there were so many centres in which similar styles were current, such as Wrockwardine in Shropshire, Yorkshire, the Newcastle district, and Alloa in Scotland, that it is an extremely difficult matter to claim with any certainty that a specimen is 'Nailsea'. On the other hand, it is doubtful whether any evidence, however positive, that the articles were made elsewhere, will have any influence on the designation 'Nailsea'.

But the mystery is a real one; less than fifty years after the works at Nailsea had finally closed its doors, imitations of the ware presumed to have been made there, were on the market. As early as 1911, St George Gray[1] wrote: 'Fabrications of Nailsea Glass (sometimes excellent imitations) specially prepared for the unwary collector, are already on the market. Some of the most flagrant imitations offered for sale (perhaps more in the neighbourhood of Bristol than elsewhere) are copies of splashed Nailsea glass, especially those pieces in the form of long-necked bottles.'

The factory was founded in 1788 by John Robert Lucas (1754–1828), son of a Bristol bottle manufacturer. During the years of its existence there were numerous changes of ownership, but the business grew to one of some importance. For a period it was under the control of Robert Lucas Chance, who in 1824 acquired the famous Spon Lane works at Birmingham.

The Nailsea glasshouses occupied a site of over five acres, some of the old buildings still standing. In 1856 the works were described as being on a large scale for the manufacture of crown and sheet glass, and a few years later there were some 350 workmen engaged there. The works ceased to function in 1873, mainly due to the difficulty in obtaining coal of the requisite quality.

During its period of operation, the works were engaged entirely in the manufacture of sheet glass. From a careful study made quite recently of existing records, no positive evidence has been found that any coloured glass was ever made there. The debris of the factory has been examined, and specimens of the Nailsea pale green transparent glass as used for windows are in several collections, but no colours have so far been unearthed.

There is also no evidence that any bottles were made there. Bottles were made, however, at a neighbouring works at Stanton Drew, some six miles from Bristol, which, in the early years of the Nailsea factory, belonged to the company. It is, therefore, not inconceivable that the flecked and festooned ware was made at Stanton Drew, but took the name of the parent company, i.e. Nailsea.

Reports of interviews with men who actually worked at Nailsea are conflicting. Some claimed that much of the ornamental ware was made at Bristol, others that articles were brought to Nailsea by workmen who came from Birmingham, and that ornamental glass was made by the men in their spare time as *tours de force*. It is, indeed, known that a few years before the works were closed, a small furnace was built to make 'fancy' goods, such as propagators, cucumber glasses, rolling pins and glass shades.

[1] H. St George Gray, *Connoisseur*, June 1911, Vol. XXX, pp. 85–98.

There is a record of Timothy Warren who served his apprenticeship in glass-making at Nailsea, and who later travelled north, first to Newcastle-on-Tyne, where he owned a glasshouse in St Thomas Street, and later to Alloa in Scotland, where he finally settled with his wife and family. It is known that Alloa glassworks produced articles of the type shown in Plate 6(D), the thin white opaque streaks being known as 'quillings'. The double-necked flasks of this type were claimed to be used for oil and vinegar.

Some writers claim that the ornamental ware was made by some French glass-makers who resided permanently at Nailsea; a row of cottages was built for their special colony, the block of buildings being known as 'French Rank'.

Tradition and superstition have both added their quota to the popularity of Nailsea glass. Who has not heard, for example, of the witch ball? These glass balls, the inner surface smeared and daubed with a variety of colours, are accredited to the Nailsea workmen. They were hung in their cottages, so the legend claims, to ward off the evil eye. Modern imitations, in various colours silvered on the inner surface, are not unknown.

Then there was the twisted glass rod, in the form of a walking stick, which may have been anything from four to eight feet in length. The rod was hung in a conspicuous position in the dwelling, and was carefully cleaned every morning to create a spell against certain diseases, such as malaria. This superstition was so deeply rooted that the owner could seldom be persuaded to sell one.[1] If the rod unfortunately became broken, it was said that some dire misfortune would soon be the lot of a member of the household.

Glass pole-heads are accredited to the glassmen of Nailsea. Indeed, they have been held to represent the insignia of the old Nailsea Glassworker's Guild which had its meetings in a tavern in the row of cottages in French Rank. Brass pole-heads are, of course, well known to collectors.[2] They were formerly carried by the village clubs of Somerset and parishes on its borders. A few varieties in wood are known, and an occasional one in iron, but glass specimens are exceedingly rare. They are of opaque white glass, streaked with pink and royal blue, and were probably made at Bristol.

Also described as 'Nailsea' are the peculiar love-tokens which were, indeed, made at all glassworks near coastal towns, i.e., Nailsea, Bristol, London, Sunderland and Newcastle. They were mainly useful articles such as rolling pins, scent-bottles and drinking vessels,

[1] George Soane, *Curiosities of Literature*, 1847, Vol. 1, p. 206.

[2] Sir S. Ponsonby Fane, 'Club Pole Heads in Somerset', April 1907, *Connoisseur*, Vol. XVII, pp. 256–262.

and had inscribed on them initials and dates, or an amorous verse or motto. For example, there are scent-bottles inscribed ML, 1822; SR 1822; MS, 1819; and there are rolling pins inscribed with such words as 'May the eye of the Lord watch over you', and 'Be true to me'.

Rolling pins also have a legendary background. They are generally hollow, the open end being closed by means of a cork. No doubt they were used for domestic purposes, for flour is frequently found remaining in them. An occasional specimen has a residue of common salt. It is thought that the rolling pins were filled with salt to give them weight when in use, and to keep them cool.

Reference has already been made[1] to three styles of Nailsea glass, (*a*) flecked ware, (*b*) ware crudely decorated in bold white festoons, and (*c*) a more sophisticated style with well-formed latticinio decoration. Vessels in groups (*a*) and (*b*) are much in the same style, the difference being only in the decorative treatment. One is splashed with flecks of enamel colours, and the other with bold enamel bands or festoons. The vessels themselves, however, are of the same material.

MOTTLED OR FLECKED WARE

A careful examination of specimens of the first style discloses certain common features:

(1) The flecks follow no regular pattern, but occur indiscriminately all over the surface of the vessel; measurement shows from half a dozen to two or three dozen for each square inch of surface.

(2) They vary in size and shape, from round, often faint, specks no bigger than a pin's head, to sharply defined elliptical shapes up to three-eighths of an inch in diameter. One specimen is known with a speck measuring one inch long by one and seven-eighths inches wide.

(3) The colours are predominantly opaque white, with a distinct bluish tinge. The white flecks are relieved by a sprinkling of opaque specks of other colours such as sealing-wax red, bright yellow, and pale sapphire-blue.

(4) All the flecks, without a single exception, are on the surface of a specimen; some stand out in relief, especially in the case of the larger ones.

(5) The flecks are often 'crazed', that is, the surface is covered with fine cracks or fissures sometimes seen on the glaze of old pottery. The enamel glass from which the flecks are made is obviously quite different in composition from that of the green glass body.

[1] See p. 49.

It is easy to hazard a guess as to why and how this flecked ware came to be manufactured. First, the duty imposed by the Excise Act of 1745 of one penny per pound by weight of the raw materials used in the making of flint glass had been doubled in 1777, and again increased ten years later. When the Nailsea works commenced operations, the tax was nearly $2\frac{1}{2}$d per pound by weight on flint glass. The duty on green bottle-glass, however, was only roughly one-fifth of this amount. In order to avoid the tax, therefore, it is likely that some of the simple domestic ware was made in bottle-glass, probably at Stanton Drew, but to give its rather drab nature an appeal, mottled decoration in the form of enamel flecks of colour were liberally splashed over the surface.

Enamel glass was made at Bristol, only a few miles away, and as the Nailsea Company, to whom the Stanton Drew factory belonged, had an office and warehouse in Bristol, it would have been an easy matter for the workmen to have obtained discarded pieces of enamel glass and to have crushed it ready for use.

In the making of an article with flecked decoration, some of the enamel chips would have been sprinkled over the surface of a 'marver' plate, and hot glass attached to a gathering iron rolled over them to which they would have adhered. The mass of glass was re-heated and finally blown into the required form, the enamel chips being firmly welded to the surface of the vessel.

The jug shown in Plate 6(A) is typical of this interesting group. The body is boldly flecked with white enamel and coloured blobs well distributed over both the body and the neck. This specimen is particularly well-proportioned, and is ten inches in height in typical dark green bottle-glass.

Gray[1] states that jugs of this type with splashes of colour as well as white were also made at Sunderland, Wrockwardine Wood (Salop) and Hopton Wafers. Thorpe[2] mentions that the yellow mottling seems to distinguish Wrockwardine glass from that of the Nailsea types.

The flecked ware includes jugs, two-handled vessels, rolling pins, cups, decanters and bottles. They are distinctive in style, different, indeed, from the rustic glassware made in any other part of the country. They have a charm of their own, and in some cases an agreeable symmetry that suggests the classic curves of the Roman models. This is particularly noticeable in some of the two-handled urns. Although the craftsmanship is of a high order, the finish is

[1] H. St George Gray, *op. cit.*

[2] W. A. Thorpe, *A History of English and Irish Glass* (London, 1929), Vol. i, p. 28.

rough; there was never any attempt to apply the delicate touches so characteristic, for example, of the Newcastle craftsmen.

BOTTLE-GREEN WARE DECORATED WITH ENAMEL FESTOONS

Another style accredited to the Nailsea factory are the articles crudely decorated in bold white festoons, such as the specimens B and C, Plate 6. The jug (B) is in the collection of Sir Hugh Chance, whose ancestor, Robert Lucas Chance, controlled for a time the factory at Nailsea. The jug is definitely Nailsea. It is three and a half inches in height, and is encircled with broad bands in white opal. The jug (C), in the same collection, is four and a half inches in height, and is in the similar smoky green glass. There is a white opal rim, but no other decoration. This specimen cannot with the same certainty be ascribed to Nailsea.

There are two distinct styles of this crude latticinio decoration; those of the same material, form and standard of quality as the flecked ware (Plate 6, B and C), and another style, the more expertly finished ware in either flint, pale green glass, and more rarely in dark blue glass. Examples are D, E and F in Plate 6. From an examination of the two styles, it is evident that the second type belongs to quite a different class; there is a quality of finish that is obviously an attempt to set a higher standard of appeal, and the ware is fashioned with more attention to detail. The agreeable symmetry and crude beauty so characteristic of the first style, however, are absent.

It has been suggested by more than one writer that the second style of latticinio ware was made by French and Venetian workmen, who moved from one glass factory to another as necessity required. These artisans travelled the country, and would work in a centre so long as their ware sold well; when the local demand was satisfied, they moved elsewhere.

Although most of the latticinio is in opaque white, a furnace for the making of this particular glass at the centre of operations was not essential. The foreign glass-makers would have carried with them sticks of opaque glass such as was made at Bristol and Lambeth. They would have used a similar method for the making of a flask or bottle, in latticinio, for example, as was used for the making of a wineglass with opaque-twist stem. A number of short lengths of canes of opaque white glass would be set round the inner corrugated surface of a cylindrical mould or cup. The whole mass was heated and a soft blob of molten flint-glass attached to a gathering iron dropped into the mould. After cooling slightly, the blob of glass was withdrawn, the white opaque canes having become firmly attached to its surface. The whole was then reheated, and the glass manipulated by the usual process of marvering, stretching and blowing into the shape required. The white canes would follow the flow lines of the glass as it was being worked, into all manner of intricate and fascinating patterns. This latticinio method of decoration was perfected by the Venetians, who produced many intricate patterns and variations from the sixteenth century onwards.

COLOURED WARE WITH CRUDE LATTICINIO DECORATION

There were many articles produced with the latticinio style of decoration. Some have already been mentioned as being more decorative than functional, such as large pipes, shoes, bells and bellows; but some of the flasks, for which Nailsea has built up a reputation, were no doubt quite useful articles. It is recorded that they were used by visitors taking the waters at Bath. It is probable that they were used for carrying wine and other refreshments during the wearisome journeys in the saddle and by coach.

The flasks vary from three and a half to ten and a half inches in height, and some have two separate compartments and two necks, making them suitable for two different liquids. They vary in colour from the transparent body with regular loops and festoons in white opaque glass (Plate 6, D) to flasks with blue or white opaque bodies with festoons of pink. The rarer colours are yellow and dark red.

The stoppered decanters in latticinio were obviously not made at Nailsea; neither were the glass bells in various colours, although specimens were found in the Nailsea district. One specimen in the Taunton Museum has a ruby bell, a clapper in clear white glass, the handle a greenish opaque white and the top peacock blue. Another has a bell of clear white glass with latticinio work in opaque white, the clapper clear white, and the handle cobalt blue. Another large bell is of ruby glass with pale blue streaks, the handle clear white, while another is opaque white with pink loops, the handle being bright green.

Pots of glass of these various colours, ruby, opaque white, peacock blue, cobalt blue, opaque pink, bright green, as well as clear white, would have had to be available for the manufacture of these articles; they are, therefore, much more likely to have been made at some other centre, such as Stourbridge, Birmingham, or Bristol.[1]

[1] See p. 60.

CHAPTER FIVE

Bristol Glass

BRISTOL will always be assured of an honourable place in records of English art for its eighteenth-century ceramics. Delftware had already been made there in the seventeenth century, and early in the eighteenth century the Bristol artists gave promise of their future renown by creating decorative styles for delft that had a character of their own, quite different, indeed, from the Chinese influence which prompted them.

Just before the middle of the eighteenth century, the Bristol potters turned their attention to porcelain, and the connection between the porcelain made at Lowdin's glasshouse at Redcliff Backs and the famous porcelain factory at Worcester is now well established. Bristol, too, was the seat of English experiments during the second half of the eighteenth century to reproduce the hard-paste porcelain that had for so many centuries remained a secret of the Chinese potters. It is only to be expected, therefore, at a centre where an intense interest in ceramics had been long shown, that attention should be given to glass-making.

Bristol is well known today among collectors for its opaque white glass decorated in enamel colours, its famous dark blue glass — indeed, any specimen of dark blue glass is today immediately dubbed Bristol — and, to a lesser extent, its bright green glass. Many other colours have been accredited from time to time to Bristol, but there is no positive evidence that glass of any other colour was made there. The Bristol glass-makers also specialized in gilding and in glass-cutting. It is probable that the popularity of Bristol in the eighteenth century was due more to its high-quality cut and engraved crystal glass, than to its coloured varieties.

The earliest record of a glasshouse occurs in 1651, and by the end of the seventeenth century there were no less than nine in operation; Bristol even at that time ranked fourth in this country in importance in glass production. Its importance can be judged by the fact that early in the eighteenth century, when the town was honoured by a Royal visit, glass-makers took a prominent part, according to the notice in the *Daily Post* of November 14, 1738: 'Bristol November 11th. Yesterday the Prince and Princess of Wales paid their promised visit to the City. . . . The Companies of the City made a magnificent appearance in their formalities, marching two by two, preceding the Corporation and the Royal Guests. The Company of Glassmen went first, dressed in Holland shirts, on horseback, some with swords, others with crown and sceptres in their hands made of glass.'

Bristol glassmen were again accorded Royal patronage later in the century when Isaac Jacobs, a Bristol manufacturer, was made glass-maker to George III.

OPAQUE WHITE GLASS

In spite of the wide selection of decorative effects that were available to the Bristol glass-maker, there is no doubt it is to the opaque white glass made there, that Bristol owes much of its renown for glass.

The art of making dense white glass of the appearance of modern china, or of a more translucent variety which can best be described as milk-white, has been known from the earliest times. Egyptian opaque white glass was found in excavations in the island of Elephantine and is estimated to date from the second or first centuries B.C. This ancient glass was found on analysis to be essentially of the same composition as the modern commercial product.

In spite of this early application, however, it was not until the middle of the eighteenth century that the English glass-maker made extensive use of opaque white glass, and, indeed, it is still a controversial point as to where and when it first occurred. It is agreed, however, that its use in this country was suggested by Continental practice, and that it enjoyed a brief period of fashion between the Excise Acts of 1745 and 1777, at which later date opaque white was considered of sufficient importance to provide an increased revenue, and was therefore included in the tax.

Earlier in the century, the English glass-maker had achieved great success with air-twist decoration, in which fine threads of air were drawn in a variety of patterns in the stems of such vessels as drinking glasses, candlesticks and sweetmeat-glasses. Later, the threads of air were replaced with threads of opaque white, and that the new technique was quickly mastered is shown by the great variety of patterns that exist. In the small confine of the stems of drinking glasses, for example, the glass-maker so combined and permutated simple threads of opaque white glass that nearly one hundred and fifty distinct varieties are known. Many of these, it is thought, were made at Bristol.

Vessels formed entirely of opaque white, however, were not

made in this country to any extent, although they were known on the Continent in the seventeenth century. John Greene imported opaque white glass from the Venetian glass-maker, Morelli, between 1666 and 1673; an item in the form of a vase in imitation of porcelain was among his specifications. The German glass-makers also produced opaque white glass known as *Porcellein-Glas*, and articles such as porringers, cream-pots and vinegar cruets were imported into this country.[1]

Towards the close of the eighteenth century many objects were being made in opaque white in various parts of the country, but on the whole it cannot be said that the material itself ever reached a high standard of quality. The early types varied from dense, stony white which was really opaque, to a translucent, opalescent glass having the fiery characteristics of the opal when the light was transmitted through it, and a milk-and-water appearance with reflected light. Nevertheless, in spite of the variation in opacity, there was an increasing demand for this type of glass. Keepsake mugs were popular, for sale at country fairs, and rolling pins, figures and many other kinds of fancy glass, such as glass-workers might have devised in their spare time, were vessels which found a ready market. Many of these were painted in enamel colours and fired, but often they were left unfired, when the painted decoration gradually wore off.

The opaque white glass made at Bristol, however, was quite different in composition and character from that made elsewhere. It was denser in texture and more creamy white than that from other centres, in fact more like fine Chinese stoneware or porcelain in appearance. Its close resemblance to this material is not surprising when it is considered that it was developed where experiments with delft and porcelain had been conducted, and where the manufacture of these materials had become established on a commercial scale.

Bristol opaque white was a potash-lead glass containing a higher proportion of lead, indeed, than ordinary transparent flint glass; the opacifying medium was oxide of tin. The relatively high lead and low silica content caused it to be very soft, and also gave it its high density.

It would appear that the first glasshouse in Bristol to make it was 'The Redcliff Backs Glasshouse', not far from St Mary's Church and adjoining the pottery at Redcliff Backs. It is recorded that candlesticks in opaque white were made there in 1757,[2] and there are

[1] R. Dossie, *Handmaid to the Arts* (London 1st Ed., 1758), Vol. ii, p. 312.
[2] F. Buckley, *Glass*, Vol. viii, p. 278.

entries in the ledger of this glasshouse of the painter Michael Edkins concerning his work between 1762 and 1767.

MICHAEL EDKINS

Edkins had a colourful career. He left Birmingham to try his luck in Bristol shortly before 1755, for in that year he married Elizabeth, daughter of William James, glassmaker. He at first found work as a painter of coaches, but later was employed in decorating delftware, and blue and opaque white glass. Edkins found continuous employment at the Redcliff Backs Glasshouse between 1762 and 1787 during its several changes of ownership, and at the Temple Street Glasshouse between 1785 and 1787.[1]

The styles favoured by Edkins are now fairly well established, as specimens of his work were fortunately preserved by his relatives. Birds and flowers such as are shown on the cruet bottles in Plate 7 (A, B and C) are typical of his work. Chinese subjects were a favourite choice of the Bristol painters of delftware and porcelain, and it is not an easy matter to distinguish the work of one artist from that of another. There are unfortunately no signed and dated specimens of Edkins's work, such as those decorated in enamel by the Beilby family of Newcastle-on-Tyne.

From records, it is known that Edkins painted both opaque white and blue glass articles, such as vases, quart mugs, cruets, tea-caddies, candlesticks, basins and jars. The vases decorated with fanciful Chinese figures and exotic birds are much valued by collectors.

A specimen is shown in Plate 7(F). It is in Chinese *famille-rose* style with a Chinese lady and mandarin, the latter wearing a feather in his broad-brimmed hat; just out of vision is a boy to the left of the lady. All three have long, pointed finger nails. On the reverse is a river scene with a boat having a single sail, and, in the near distance, buildings and hillocks. The vase is six and a half inches high, and is painted in bright enamel colours.

This vase is typical of the Bristol opaque white enamel-painted ware, but other forms are met with. One which changed hands recently can be described as bottle-shaped, of globular form with slender cylindrical neck and trumpet mouth, its height eight and a half inches. The neck was enamelled in a pale palette with sprays of pink cabbage roses, hyacinths, tulips and single leaves.

Candlesticks and tapersticks are also found in opaque white decorated with enamel. The candlesticks are usually between nine

[1] See p. 61.

and ten inches in height, the incised twist shaft having a multi-ring collar at each end terminating in a domed foot. The socket and foot are usually painted with bouquets, sprays of garden flowers and butterflies. An occasional candlestick of this style has a nozzle in Battersea enamel. The tapersticks are between six and seven inches in height and are *en suite* with the candlesticks.

The subject of opaque white glass cannot be left without further reference to the streaked ware already discussed under Nailsea glass. The more sophisticated style of latticinio was most probably made at Bristol, especially those articles with a base of transparent, almost colourless glass, or the dark blue glass usually accredited to Bristol. Those articles with latticinio work in opaque pink and other colours were also most probably of Bristol origin, although the style will always be associated with the name of Nailsea.

BLUE GLASS

Articles in dark blue cobalt glass are today always presumed to have been made at Bristol. It is, of course, correct that it was made there —so much has been established from documentary records; but this same glass was also made at other centres long after Bristol ceased to be a glass-making centre. Just after the middle of the eighteenth century blue glass was made in London, Stourbridge, Newcastle, Sunderland and Warrington, and indeed, its manufacture became fairly general throughout the country by the end of the century.

Only a few articles in blue glass can with any certainty be assigned to Bristol. Blue decanters, for example, with long, slender necks, pear-shaped bodies and lozenge-shaped stoppers with bevelled edges, such as that shown in Plate 7(D), were most probably made at Bristol. A somewhat similar shape, but made in flint glass, was chosen by the Belfast glass-makers, and, indeed became a characteristically distinguishing feature of decanters from that centre. This fact is easily established today because many of these decanters are marked 'B. Edwards, Belfast'.

Benjamin Edwards, who left England in 1776 because of the iniquitous regulations of the Excise Act to found a glassworks in Belfast, had originally been a glass-maker in Bristol. It is not unreasonable to assume that he introduced the shape into Ireland that had been popular in Bristol, for decanters of similar style were not made at either Waterford or Cork.

The Jacobs, father and son, who had their glasshouse in Temple Street, Bristol, also specialized in blue glass, and fortunately several signed specimens are extant which make it easily possible to recognize this particular Bristol style.

Isaac Jacobs has already been referred to[1] as being made glassmaker to George III. His father, Lazarus Jacobs, had been a glassmaker before him, and had founded the glasshouse in Temple Street, Bristol. He had established a good business in glass-cutting and engraving, and between the years 1785 and 1787 employed the artist Michael Edkins to decorate his glass in enamel colours.[2] It is well established from entries in his ledger that Edkins painted blue glass; for example, 'one pint blue can ornamented with gold and letters', and 'to three pr. blue cornicopios ornamented with gold'.

It is most probable that the glass chosen for such decoration was the dark blue glass known to have been made at the Temple Street glasshouse, for there are one or two specimens in this colour with gilt decoration signed on the back in gold 'I. Jacobs, Bristol'. A dark blue wine-glass cooler is shown on Plate 7(E). It has a gilt key-fret border and is signed 'I. Jacobs, Bristol'. The signature is shown below. The Jacobs also specialized in blue glass decanters provided

with gilt chain and label suspended from the neck, some of which are also signed in gold.

Blue toilet-bottles can also with some certainty be ascribed to Bristol. There is a record, for example, of two blue and gold toilet-bottles in a list of stolen property in the *Bristol Journal*, October 15, 1763. The gold-mounted scent-bottle shown in Plate 7(G) is typical of the Bristol style. It is painted in enamel colours in the fanciful style favoured by Michael Edkins. The patch-box, Plate 7(H), in in similar style.

GREEN GLASS

Bright green glass was most probably made at Bristol; specimens are extant of scent-bottles similar in style and decoration to the blue ones already described. This green glass, of a distinctive and deep colour, was made before the Glass Excise Act of 1745; some writers, indeed, class specimens as of the seventeenth century. It was made at various centres, but it is unlikely that the Bristol variety was

[1] See p. 57.　　　[2] See p. 59.

made before the middle of the eighteenth century. The ribbed grips
of the swords in the Bristol Museum are of this dark green metal.
Early bright green drinking glasses, now rare, usually followed the
German *roemer* in style, but cannot be described as Bristol.

GILDING

In addition to enamelling, the Bristol artists also employed gilding
for decorative purposes. Michael Edkins and the Jacobs both used it
on blue glass. No doubt the process was developed from that employed at Bristol for firing the enamel decoration. According to
Owen,[1] the coloured enamel frit was 'vitrified in a muffler or kiln'.
The Bristol gilded glasses were decorated in the same manner,
although some specimens are extant with oil-gilt decoration. The
oil-gilt or varnish-gilt method was used in the first half of the century to gild wheel-engraving, but went out of fashion about 1770
when it was superseded by burnished gilding.

CUT AND ENGRAVED GLASS

Bristol was probably more famous in the eighteenth century for its
high-quality flint glass than for its coloured variety. In the second
half of the eighteenth century many notices appeared in Bristol
newspapers of 'all sorts of cut, flowered and plain glass of the newest
and best patterns'. In one notice in the *Bristol Journal,* March 12,
1774, the items mentioned for sale included 'Wine, Beer, Water,
Jelly and a variety of plain as well as other curious cut Flint glasses,
Decanters, Cans, Dobbins, Tumblers, Fruit Dishes, Candlesticks,
Salts, Cruets, Castors, Mustard Pots, Patty Pans and Cream Jugs;
Dram Gooseberry, Phial and neat-cut Smelling Bottles'.

The style of cutting about this period is furnished by a trade card[2]
of Wadham Ricketts & Co, who owned the Phoenix Glassworks in
Bristol. The card shows a bowl with a deeply scalloped rim, a band
of relief diamonds on the upper part of the body, and flutes on the
lower half to the base. There is also a candelabrum with curved
arms decorated with pendent drops, and swags of pendent lustres
suspended from a canopy at the top of a notched spire. A similar
candelabrum is shown in Plate 8(E). Candelabra of this style could
easily have been of Bristol origin.

[1] Hugh Owen, *Two Centuries of Ceramic Art in Bristol* (London, 1873), p. 380.
[2] *Dix Collection of Newscuttings*, Bristol Library.

CHAPTER SIX

Illuminating Glassware

BEFORE the advent of such civilized refinements as gas and electricity with which to lighten the dark hours, cottages and mansions alike were lighted with either rushes or candles in metal holders, or with metal oil lamps. It was not until the discovery of Ravenscroft's glass-of-lead medium in 1676 that glass articles for illumination, such as lamps, candlesticks and, later, candelabra and chandeliers, began to replace the earlier metal holders.

The properties of the new glass medium were ideal for this purpose, for its transparency and powers of light dispersion caused it to be a fascinating novelty even in daylight hours, but at night, the long slender arms of candelabra and chandeliers, with their countless facets gleaming from the light of numerous candles must have appeared in those early days an even greater spectacle of delight.

GLASS LAMPS

One of the earliest forms of glass lamps was the 'lanthorn', a metal chamber-lamp with glass sides and holding a candle. Their use was rather different from that of candlesticks, for they were intended to be carried about the house, and used in a manner for which an expensive candlestick was clearly out of place. Moreover, they could be used out of doors, and were claimed at the time to be much safer than candlesticks, an important point to be taken into consideration when the risk of fire was a matter of the gravest concern.

The earliest glass lamps were in light green window-glass, but before the end of the seventeenth century, that is, immediately after the discovery of Ravenscroft's glass medium, much improvement had taken place in their manufacture. Glass plates were already being supplied ground and polished,[1] and hanging lamps with sides of polished plate-glass were being used in the halls and passages of the best houses.

Probably the earliest notice of glass chamber-lamps occurs just before the change of the century in the *London Gazette*, October 30, 1693: 'Glass Lanthorns, finely painted to burn candles in, for Halls, etc from 4s. to £10. William Fells, tin-man, in King Street.'

Lanterns and chamber-lamps, it is seen, belonged more to the

[1] See p. 74.

domain of the tinsmith and metal-worker than to that of the glass-maker. They obtained their glass from the grinder and polisher of glass plates, who also supplied the coach builder and the maker of looking glasses. It is evident from the above notice that even in those days glass chamber-lamps could be expensive, and therefore elaborate, articles.

The use of glass oil-lamps also began to grow rapidly, and there is no doubt they were made and used in large numbers as household utensils. Their development must have been rapid, for in 1735 they were sufficiently improved to be capable of burning for forty hours without refilling.

Improvements were made in other ways. The original glass lamp was a flattened globe of glass provided with a hole in the top through which the wick was inserted; it was mounted on a stem and foot, and was usually provided with a handle on the stem. A typical early eighteenth-century glass lamp is shown in Plate 8(A). The later improved types had a large concave collar or 'drip dish' below the globe, for catching stray drops of oil.

Still later, the idea occurred to increase the lighting power of the lamp by having more than one wick holder. For this purpose the stem of the earlier simple type was discarded, and the body was shaped to vase form, and provided with several branches. In effect, they looked something like a tea-pot with two or three spouts. They were fitted in most cases with handles. A specimen is shown in Plate 8(B). Early in the second half of the century, they were cut and engraved, but unfortunately few such specimens have survived the test of time.

GLASS CLOCK-LAMPS

About 1730 lamps began to be used for purposes other than lighting, for example, as a means for telling the time in the dark. In most houses, the only means of getting a light at night to tell the time was with flint and steel. It can be well appreciated that to do this by such means in the middle of the night in a draughty chamber was no pleasant or simple task, and the clock lamp must have been a great boon at the time.

The glass-maker and the tinsmith co-operated in the manufacture of these ingenious devices. They were made partly of brass and partly of glass, and were in great demand at the time. The oil was stored in a tall glass tube at the top of the lamp, the wick-holder protruding from one side; the time was told by the sinking of the oil in the tube, which was marked outside by 'hour' degrees. A

11. CHIMNEY-GLASS AND IRISH MIRRORS

A: Chimney-glass with three mirrors and painting after Hondekoeter. B: Irish mirror with frame made up of facets of coloured glass. A small chandelier is suspended in front of the mirror. C: Irish mirror with scroll base and faceted glass frame. (*A: Messrs Mallett & Son Ltd; B, C: Mr Cecil Davis.*)

12. DRINKING GLASSES, 17TH AND 18TH CENTURIES

A: Baluster glass, late 17th century. B: Wineglass with air-twist stem, mid-18th century (*Victoria and Albert Museum*). C: Glass with white opaque twist stem, third quarter of the 18th century (*Messrs Arthur Churchill*). D: Wineglass with faceted stem, last quarter of the 18th century. E: Rummer typical of the style at the change of the 18th century. F: Flute glass used for ratafia or similar cordial, second half of the 18th century.

specimen is shown in Plate 8(c). This type of 'clock lamp' was described in *The Craftsman*, December 19, 1730, as follows: 'Ashburne's New Invented Clock-Lamp, showing the Hours of the Night exactly as they pass; far exceeding anything of this kind ever yet invented. Are sold by the Inventor and Maker, Leonard Ashburne, at the Sugar Loaf in Paternoster Row, Cheapside, at 6s. each.'

Another interesting advertisement appeared a few months later in *The Craftsman*, February 27, 1731: 'Walker's original new-invented Clock-Lamp. Being a most compleat machine and so artfully contrived that it shows the Hours of the Night exactly as they pass; supplying at once the place of a Clock, Watch and Candle, and has been approv'd by the most Ingenious. 'Tis managed with so little trouble and so very neatly that it neither daubs the fingers nor the place where it stands, as others do. In short, hardly any Person that has occasion to keep a light in the night, if they knew the conveniency of them would ever be without one.'

CANDLESTICKS

The earliest types of candlesticks in glass belong to the seventeenth century. They are fairly light in construction, with hollow knopped stems and pedestal feet, and were probably inspired by the French lace-makers' lamps of the period, for many of them are elongated versions of those vessels. The lace-makers' lamps, also known as *orineaux*, were glass globes filled with water which acted as a condensing lens for the light, either from rush or candle, to concentrate the beam on the pillow of lace.

Before the end of the seventeenth century, however, candlesticks began to follow their counterparts in metal, and the styles adopted were evidently greatly influenced by them. The hollow stem gave place to a solid knopped one, in which the true and inverted baluster motifs were popular decorative features. The feet were much more practical in these later candlesticks. They added more to the stability of the article by being wider in proportion to the height, and were made considerably heavier. Domed feet, both plain and terraced, were popular styles.

New styles were introduced after the accession in 1714 of George I to the English Throne. The English glass-maker had by this time mastered the properties of the glass-of-lead of Ravenscroft, and he began to coax his medium into more pleasing and symmetrical shapes. The candlestick of this period (1714–25) was supplied with a ribbed and beaded candle-socket mounted on a Silesian shouldered stem, with an annulated knop consisting of triple rings. The foot was domed, with radial ribs to match the candle-socket. Candle-sticks of the first quarter of the eighteenth century were much more useful and robust articles than those of the previous century.

Candlesticks were decorated by air beads and air twists during the first half of the century. A style sometimes seen is a column with either a spiral cable or multiple air twist collared with tear-drop knops at each extremity. The foot is wide and usually domed, and may be either terraced or ribbed. Candle-sockets were usually plain and cylindrical, but an occasional deviation from this style is found with a bulbous finish where it joins the column, giving it a thistle shape. Opaque twist styles are known in candlesticks, but did not remain fashionable long before they were superseded by the cut variety. Opaque white candlesticks were made at Bristol, some being painted in enamel colours.[1]

It is to be expected that decoration by cutting would not have been long delayed in glass candlesticks. Chandeliers had already begun to receive the attention of the glass-cutter — 'Crystal Cut Lustres' had been advertised in 1728 — and the application of this new form of decoration to such an appropriate article as a glass candlestick must have made an immediate appeal.

The earliest notice, however, did not occur until later in the century when in 1742 Jerom Johnson advertised 'diamond-cut and scalloped candlesticks'. Scalloping had been an early and popular form of decoration. It had been applied to sweetmeat glasses as early as 1722. Lady Baillie, a Scottish diarist, had described[2] a dinner party in that year in which the centre-piece of the dessert table had been 'a high scaloped glass'.

The candle-socket and occasionally the rim of the foot of the candlestick were decorated in this manner. The stem was sometimes cut in hollow-diamond fashion, that is, a series of interlacing hollows whose edges intersected to form a four- or six-sided diamond motif.

The influence of the Adam brothers began to make itself felt towards the end of the eighteenth century, and fluted columns, square-cut and terraced feet, were acknowledgments to the classical revival. They did not achieve a great deal of popularity, however, and the earlier choice of decoration remained in vogue until the candle was superseded by gas.

The Irish glasshouses specialized in candlesticks, the specimens shown in Plate 8(D), probably being Irish. The Adam influence is

[1] See p. 60.
[2] *The Household Books of Lady Grisell Baillie*, 1692–1733, Scottish History Society, Vol. i, Edinburgh, 1911.

shown in the square bases and urn-shaped stems. Candlesticks of this period were practical affairs; not only were they made in squat form with heavy bases to give them stability, but the candle-sockets were removable, which made the replacing of the candles a comparatively simple operation.

TEA CANDLESTICKS, TAPERSTICKS OR TAPERS

These articles were similar in style to the ordinary candlestick, but were made to a much smaller model; they were usually between five and seven inches in height. The height rarely exceeded seven inches, but some tapersticks are known of less than five inches. Knopped, air-beaded and air-twist styles, opaque twist and cut varieties are known, being exact counterparts of the candlesticks of the same period.

The precise use of the eighteenth-century taperstick appears to be in some doubt. Christopher Haedy advertised in *The Bath Chronicle*, November 20, 1766: 'The stock in trade of a German who was the first that brought the art of cutting and engraving from Germany. Consisting of great variety of Cut, Engraved and Gilt glasses — Tea and other Candlesticks.' The same glass-maker later advertised in *The Bath and Bristol Chronicle*, November 20, 1768: 'To be sold by hand at the Sadler's Arms in Bath the stock in trade of a glass cutter from London, consisting of a great variety of cut engraved and gilt glasses — cut Candlesticks, Tapers, with a choice collection of articles for Chimney-pieces.'

There are two schools of thought on the question of the tea candlestick and the taperstick. Buckley[1] suggests that the 'tea candlesticks' advertised by Haedy in 1766 are probably equivalent to his 'Tapers' in the advertisement of 1768. If this view is accepted, the use of these narrow-socketed candlesticks is explained; they were designed for the tea- or side-table. Tea drinking had, of course, by this time, become firmly established in this country, and a small candle capable of burning for a short period may have been used in conjunction with the tea set. The candlestick used would have been described as a 'tea candlestick'.

On the other hand, some writers claim that 'Tapers' was a contracted name for the taperstick, which was a small counterpart of the candlestick used for holding the tapers for lighting the candles. Some of the tapersticks were provided with a grease-pan at the top of the socket, which would appear to support their use as small candlesticks. The presence of the grease-pan, however, may have

[1] F. Buckley, *History of Old English Glass*, London 1925, p. 102.

been to maintain the form similar to that of the candlestick, as many of the earlier tapersticks had plain sockets.

THE VASE CANDLESTICK

These articles were first advertised in 1777 by Christopher Haedy. They appeared in the same list as girandoles, and it is therefore probable that they did not refer to candelabra as we understand them today.

The vase candlestick was a heavy affair, all the demands for stability, and therefore, safety, being well catered for. The article was provided with a heavy metal stand, usually square like a box, with pedestal base and terraced top, on which was mounted the glass candlestick itself. In response to the classical influence, the stems followed the shape of the Grecian urn, and were cut in hollow-diamond pattern. Candle-sockets were scalloped with a star-cut grease-pan from which were suspended pendent lustres. At best, the vase candlestick cannot be regarded as particularly pleasing in style, but it remained a popular article for some time; indeed, some were shown at the Great Exhibition of 1851.

CANDELABRA

According to the trade notices, glass candelabra did not become fashionable until cutting was well established. Indeed, it was not until 1766 that we find the first mention by Christopher Haedy, a London glass-cutter, of the branched candlestick in glass, or girandole, as it was then termed. This did not in any way supersede the simple candlestick, although the latter became rather more elaborate towards the end of the century.

Meanwhile, candelabra had become firmly established in popularity. Earlier forms consisted essentially of the foot, the shaft, and the branches carrying the candle-sockets. Very quickly, the shaft was lengthened to increase the proportion of the height to width, and this step in development greatly improved the general balance and effectiveness of the design. Candelabra of this period — 1770 — to the end of the century were more stately and dignified than those of any other, a quality achieved without elaborate or over-emphasized decoration.

The earlier grease-pans had plain circular rims, but they were replaced in the later style by star-shaped pans in acknowledgment to the Adam influence. In addition, the candelabra were decorated with simple chains of pendent lustres, stars, crescents, spires and other motifs. There were also a curved device, known as a 'snake', springing from the knop carrying the branches, and a canopy at the top of the shaft, both of which were anchorages for additional pendent lustres. A specimen of this period is shown in Plate 8(E).

These pendent drops were at first sparingly applied. In the 1770 period, for example, they were little in evidence, but a few years later, when cutting became more general, advantage was taken by the cutter of every inch of space for embellishment by the wheel.

Towards the end of the century, decorative devices such as snakes and spires, which had marked the earlier rococo style, were discarded, and a more orderly and symmetrical note was evident in the general plan. Regular fringes of lustres were the dominant feature of the decoration, and cutting was on a modest scale, except for the candle-sockets and grease-pans, which were exquisitely fashioned and richly cut.

By the Regency period, the elaborate arms had degenerated into mere connecting links between the shaft and the branches, and the only decoration was a fringe of sparkling lustres which hung from the candle-sockets in such close formation that the arms were almost completely masked (Plate 8, F).

SCONCES

In the mid-eighteenth century a sconce was described as a lantern or candlestick with a screen to protect the light from the wind, or a bracket candlestick to fasten against a wall.

Glass sconces had been known in Venice early in the seventeenth century, and their development went hand in hand with the Venetian chandelier. The glass wall-plate to which the branches were attached had the edges ground and cut in diamond pattern. This style was copied by the English cutters before the beginning of the eighteenth century, although the earliest reference to them is in the *London Post*, March 31, 1704: 'Stolen, a pair of glass sconces, one of which was cracked through the middle, and ingraven.'

In *The Daily Courant*, July 29, 1724, there appeared a notice that 'James Welch, Glass-Grinder and Looking-Glass Maker, at his Warehouse behind the Rose and Crown, a Grocer's in the Broadway, Black-Fryar, London, where you may be furnished Wholesale or Retale with great variety of Peer, Chimney, or Sconce Glasses, fine Dressing-Glasses, Coach, Chariot, or Chair-Glasses, with Plate Sash-Glasses'.

It is evident from a study of the early descriptions that in most cases a glass sconce referred to a small mirror furnished with branches for holding candles. It was not necessary, however, for the glass sconce to be provided with mirror-backing. The two specimens in Plate 9(A and C) were intended to be used without a mirror. These are delightful pieces showing design and craftsmanship of a high order. The specimen A is three feet six inches in height, and that marked C is three feet high by eighteen inches in width.

Many pier-glasses and chimney-glasses were provided with sockets for fixing the candle branches, but they did not then become glass sconces or even *large* glass sconces. There is evidence of this in a notice appearing in *The Daily Courant*, July 19, 1727: 'All sorts of fine large Glass and Gold Pier glasses and Walnut-tree ditto, Chimney-Glasses, and fine large Sconces and small ones.'

Glass sconces with mirror-backing would have been more popular than sconces in metal, such as silver or brass, because of their properties of reflection. They are, however, comparatively uncommon today. When gas succeeded the candle as the main illuminant, they went out of fashion, and would, no doubt, have been destroyed, for they would have had little value as mirrors because of their size. Pier-glasses and chimney-glasses provided with branches and candle-sockets have not suffered the same fate, for they have always been both functional and decorative.

CHANDELIERS

Hanging lamps decorated with glass, such as Saracenic mosque lamps, have been known from the earliest times, but the origin of the chandelier, as we understand the term today, is obscure. They were certainly known in Venice in the seventeenth century, and, in this regard, it is significant that the importation of hanging lamps from Greece was prohibited in Venice as early as the beginning of the seventeenth century. Gerspach[1] informs us that seventeenth-century chandeliers played an important part in the decoration of Venetian salons: '*Le soir, le lustre de Venise allumé est un rayonnement harmonieux sans reflets discordants; le jour, stalactite ciselée, il égaye l'appartement comme une note claire et joyeuse.*'

The essential components of the early Venetian chandeliers were similar to the later English versions; the central supporting shaft, the branches for holding the candle sockets and the decoration. The only real difference between the Venetian and the English style was in the decorative effects. The Venetian craftsman favoured ornaments based on naturalistic motifs, such as leaves and flowers both in transparent glass and the opalescent variety. Chandeliers of that period were popular, decorated with full-scale bunches of grapes

[1] E. Gerspach, *L'art de la Verrerie*, Paris 1885.

and vine-leaves, specimens being preserved in the Museo Vitrario at Murano.

On the other hand, the English chandelier of the early eighteenth century had comparatively little decoration. It consisted essentially of a central shaft which was embellished along its length with large glass globes and with a bowl near the base from which sprang the branches for holding the candle-sockets.

An excellent specimen of this early period is shown in Plate 9(B). The decoration in this example is the scalloping of the branches, and the shallow cutting of the shaft and its ornaments. Grease-pans are also deeply scalloped in star pattern. There was a complete absence of hanging pendants and other decorative effects, which at a later period became a predominant partner in the components of the chandelier.

This added decoration began to be employed about the middle of the eighteenth century, and at first took the form of single suspended lustres advertised in 1756 as 'brilliant drops'. These pendent drops were sparingly applied, a chandelier with four branches having no more than a dozen such pendants, each being suspended separately from the branches, from the base of the lower bowl which carried the branches, or from the canopy, an ornament at the top of the shaft introduced about the middle of the century obviously to give the shaft a symmetrical appearance.

Somewhat later, chandeliers began to take on the flourish demanded by the rococo appeal; hanging drops were more liberally used, the branches were embellished with faceted spear-shafts or spires, and cut motifs were applied more profusely and with greater emphasis.

Shortly after 1770, the Adam influence began to make itself felt in every branch of design, and it was not without its effect on the chandelier. The central globes were modified to the shape of the classical Grecian urn, and ornaments were added to the pendent drops, such as stars and crescents. At this period decoration began to dominate the design. Chains of pendent drops, known as swags, were draped from the canopy to the branches, and the branches themselves carried suspended chains of lustres. These suspended chains eventually so obscured the branches that it was finally felt unnecessary to cut them. From about 1790, therefore, the branches were left plain.

The Regency period was marked by an even greater change. The decoration by chains of pendants became so profuse that the central shaft soon followed the same fate as the branches, and completely disappeared under a heavy mantle of sparkling lustres. A typical specimen of this period is that shown in Plate 9(D). This chandelier was originally at Wroxton Abbey, and is now at the Victoria and Albert Museum. It is six feet in height, and dated *circa* 1815. There are reputed to be 4500 separate pieces in it. The eighteen branches with attached candle-sockets and grease-pans are delicately formed and richly cut with deeply incised relief diamonds and with a fan escallop border.

At the time of the Great Exhibition, many firms in the country were manufacturing chandeliers. The Glass Excise Act had been repealed only six years before, which gave the glass manufacturer greater scope and freedom. Many of the chandeliers of this period were massive affairs, one, the famous 'Alhambra' chandelier, being no less than twenty-four feet high. They followed no particular style, but were for the most part replicas of earlier types. When gas succeeded candles as the main source of illuminant, chandeliers ceased to be made.

CHAPTER SEVEN

Glass Mirrors

THE necessity for a means to appraise one's appearance and to judge the effect of self-adornment, must have occurred from the time the first aggry bead was hung about the neck of some fair Phoenecian maid by her lover. A still pool of water, perhaps, which reflected a delighted face, gave the inspiration to man for the mirror.

Mirrors have been known for many centuries. Although those of polished metal were preferred by the Romans, glass ones were not unknown. Glass mirrors with the reflecting surface prepared from lead, tin or other metal were made in Germany and Lorraine as early as the twelfth century, and by the fifteenth century improvements in preparing sheet glass had enabled the glass-makers of Nuremberg, at that time an important glass-making centre, to earn fame with their convex mirrors. They used a process of blowing into a glass globe, while it was still hot from making, a metallic mixture with a little resin or salt-of-tartar. The globe, when cold, was cut into small round mirrors, which reflected a reduced image of the object.

It was not until the Venetians interested themselves in the making of mirrors early in the sixteenth century, however, that the business began to flourish. There is a record in 1507 of a grant of twenty years given by the Council of Ten to two glass-makers of Murano for the making of glass mirrors by a secret process that had previously been the exclusive possession of a German glasshouse.

Later in the same century the *specchiai* or mirror-makers of Venice formed themselves into a corporation. According to the regulations controlling this body, everyone claiming to be admitted had to prove his ability to flatten and polish a piece of glass, and to apply the metal-leaf backing. At that time, the Venetian mirrors were made by blowing the glass into large cylinders, which were split along their length and flattened on a heated stone. This was later known in this country as the 'broad' process.

The Venetian process was imported into this country by Sir Robert Mansell, a prominent Elizabethan glass-maker, who in 1623 brought over workmen from Venice for making mirrors. Such progress was made that, in 1676, John Evelyn, after a visit to the Duke

73

of Buckingham's glasshouse at Lambeth, made the following entry in his diary: 'To Lambeth — where they made huge vases of mettal as cleare, ponderous and thick as chrystal; also looking-glasses far larger and better than any that come from Venice'.

Evelyn spoke with some authority on glass, for he had gained a personal knowledge of Venetian quality from a visit to Murano in June 1645, when he examined the glasshouses, and selected specimens of the glasses made there, to be sent to England.

It was soon realized that the glass mirror was decorative as well as useful, and large and smoother sheets of glass were in demand. Mirrors began to be used both in this country and on the Continent for architectural purposes, for furnishing cabinets and for use in coaches.

A notable example of an early use of mirrors for architectural purposes is the *Galerie des Glaces* at Versailles, completed in 1682 by Charles le Brun. The sheets in this case measure two feet six inches by three feet six inches. They were made by the broad process, and as they were not ground and polished, they exhibit great distortion. To be successful in any of its functions, a mirror should possess as near perfect surfaces as possible both for parallelism and smoothness, and efforts were made towards the end of the seventeenth century, both in England and France, to achieve this object.

The manufacture of mirrors in this country began to improve rapidly, and by the end of the century great strides had been made in the grinding and polishing process. The earliest mention is in 1678, when there was reference to a new process for polishing, May 15, 1678: 'Patent for 14 years to John Roberts for his invention of grinding, polishing and diamonding glass plates for looking glasses, etc, by the motion of water and wheels'.[1]

'Diamonding' constituted a form of bevelling, a fact which is made clear in the following notice from *The London Gazette*, November 14, 1698: 'The Engine for grinding, polishing and cutting Looking Glass Plates (for which a Patent is granted) by which Glass is truly ground and pollished with the best black Polish, and also the Borders cut most curiously Hollow, and with a better lustre than any heretofore done'.

Not only were mirrors supplied ground and polished, and with decorative bevelling, but they had increased very much in size, as is shown from the following notice in *The London Gazette*, February 13, 1700: 'Large Looking-Glass Plates, the like never made in England before, both for size and goodness, are now made at the old

[1] *S.P.Dom*, May 15, 1678, Entry Book 51, p. 21.

Glass-house at Foxhall, known by the name of the Duke of Buckingham's Glasshouse, where all persons may be furnished with rough plates from the smallest size to those of six foot in length, and proportionate breadth, at reasonable rates'.

The increase in popularity of the mirror can be judged from the report in 1705 by John Gumley, a prominent glass-manufacturer, that 'The Trade of Looking Glass Plates is so considerably improv'd that they serve not only for Furniture and Ornament, in Her Majesty's Dominions at Home, but are likewise in great Esteem in Foreign Parts; the *Venetians* themselves buying of these *Plates*, and preferring them before their own'.

Both the Nurembergers and the Venetians had used the broad process in which cylinders of glass were blown and subsequently opened and flattened, and this was the process used in this country. It had its limitations. It was a difficult matter to obtain large plates of even thickness, and, after grinding and polishing, a large plate often had to be rejected or cut down in size, because of thinness along the edges.

To overcome these difficulties a new process was perfected in 1691 in France, by Louis Lucas de Nehou, which depended on the casting of sheets by pouring the liquid glass into large moulds or frames, smoothed while hot by rollers, and afterwards ground and polished on both surfaces.

It was not until nearly the end of the eighteenth century, when rooms became more spacious and loftier, and larger mirrors were required, that the French method of casting the glass sheets was taken up in this country. A company known as 'The British Cast Plate Glass Company' was formed in 1773, with the object of competing with the French manufacturers, who, at the time, had what amounted to almost a monopoly in the mirror trade throughout Europe.

The new company was entirely successful; indeed, in 1842 it is recorded that 'the Company has thriven beyond all expectation and precedent, so as to render the British Plate glass superior to that of any other country'.[1] The company was in existence until 1901, when it was acquired by Pilkington Brothers.

PIER-GLASSES

During the time of Queen Anne and George I, John Gumley carried on an extensive business in glass. He described himself variously as 'a proprietor of a glass house', 'Maker of looking-glass plates' and

[1] *The Illustrated Itinerary of Lancashire*, 1842.

'Cabinet-Maker', and in 1714 was selling 'Looking Glasses in Frames, and out of Frames, Coach-Glasses, Chimney Glasses, Sconces, Dressing Glasses, Union-Suits, Dressing Boxes, Swinging Glasses, Glass Schandeleres, Lanthorns, Gilt-Brockets — and the like'.

The above notice provides an excellent idea of the articles of furniture in which mirrors played an important part in the early eighteenth century: framed, ornamented mirrors for walls and over fireplaces, pier-glasses, sconces, swinging glasses for the dressing table, were some of the more popular.

In a letter from Brussels in 1708, the Duke of Marlborough asked his wife to 'direct Vanburgh to finish the breaks between the windows of the great cabinet with looking-glass'. At that time, the upright mirror, known as the pier-glass, designed to hang on the pier wall between two windows, was becoming a popular decorative feature for those who could afford such luxuries. Most eighteenth-century houses were built with the windows of the principal rooms on one side only, which caused the pier wall between the windows to be dark and obscure. A long, upright mirror hung on the pier wall at once eliminated the shadow by light reflected from the brighter parts of the room. It not only occupied a place which could serve no other useful purpose, but it also gave the illusion of space and height, an important consideration in the early part of the eighteenth century when most rooms were small and narrow.

Pier-glasses of the Queen Anne period are for this reason narrower than those of the later Georgian styles when the houses were built larger and loftier, and the pier-walls were correspondingly wider. The proportion of height to width in the time of Queen Anne was in some cases as much as four to one, whereas in the reign of George II, for example, the height of the pier-glass was between two and three times its width. In later styles, the proportion of height to width was still less.

Because of their length, early pier-glasses had necessarily to be made in two pieces, most probably due to the cost of making larger plates. This reason would appear to find support in that the longer pier-glasses, up to ten feet in length, were made in three pieces.

A comparatively large plate, however, was not an impossibility in this country at the time of Queen Anne. Plates from 'the smallest size to those six foot in length' had been advertised at the Duke of Buckingham's Glasshouse in 1700.[1] There is a pier-glass extant made in 1703 by John Gumley for the Duke of Devonshire which

[1] See p. 75.

measures sixty-eight inches by thirty-nine inches. It has cut-glass borders, and the coat of arms in applied decoration and cut effects on the cresting with John Gumley's name and the date 1703 scratched on the border. An interesting point concerning this mirror is that its reflecting properties are still perfect. Another pier-glass by John Gumley about the same size, signed and dated 1715 is at Hampton Court Palace.

The cost of such mirrors, however, would have been high. There is an item in the Royal Household accounts of 1703 — 'a large Pannel of Glass six foot 9 inches high and four foot broad £100 to be supplied to St James's Palace by Gerrit Jensen'.

Such plates were still made by the broad process in this country, and there appeared to be no desire on the part of the English glass-maker to adopt the Nehou process of casting, then being used in France. There was, of course, keen competition from that country, and cast plates were being imported, and continued to be for some years.

James Christie, a witness before a Parliamentary Committee in 1745[1] stated that 'a great quantity of French plate glass went through his hands every year; three pairs of large plates had sold for £2500 and he had heard of a pair of looking-glasses fetching £1000'.

But the English glass-maker was able to meet the demand so far as size was concerned. He made large plates and succeeded in supplying them comparatively plane and smooth by using only the centre portions. He also adopted the plan of building up large mirrors by sections of smaller plates, which greatly added to their charm. The glass-maker was not unaware of the advantage of this improvement and applied the same method to small mirrors in an endeavour to enhance their decorative value.

The decoration of the pier-glass changed as the century advanced. The early ones, such as the plates made by John Roberts in 1678 and by John Gumley in the early eighteenth century, had decorative borders of glass. Roberts was granted his patent for his invention of grinding, polishing and 'diamonding' glass plates for looking-glasses. Diamonding was achieved by cutting a series of intersecting hollows along the edges of the mirror, a diamond shape being formed at the points of intersection. I have described the process used in this early form of cutting elsewhere.[2] It was the earliest form of cut decoration and, applied to mirrors, constituted a form of bevelling.

[1] *Journal of the House of Commons*; cf. also 13, G.III, c. 38.
[2] E. M. Elville, *English and Irish Cut Glass*, London, 1953, p. 22.

This simple border quickly became elaborated into a separate frame of glass made up of sections mitred at the corners and enhanced by cut motifs. The crestings of the mirrors were also embellished in various ways, one signed by John Gumley in 1703 being decorated by the coat of arms and *fleur de lys* motifs in glass.

The glass-framed mirrors were superseded in the early years of the eighteenth century by richly carved wood frames or those decorated by gilt gesso work. Such elaborately decorated mirrors, however, were only within reach of the most wealthy, and the cabinet-makers, quickly realizing the potential market for such a useful article as the pier-glass, were, by 1720, supplying them at a cost within reach of the more modest purses. Plain, moulded frames of veneered walnut with crestings or hoods in pierced styles competed in this new market with simple gilt gesso frames.

Gesso was popular until 1730 or thereabouts, and, again no doubt because of cost, was superseded by frames of carved giltwood with wave moulding which, in various styles dictated by fashion, held the popular market throughout the century. Architectural designs were in demand after gesso had lost its appeal, and this style in its turn was succeeded by rococo, Chinese and Gothic as the popular taste changed.

Pier-glasses from this period are shown in Plate 10 (A–D). The specimen A is one of a pair of carved and gilt wood Chippendale pier-glasses designed by William Ince[1] and illustrated by him. Another of the same period is shown at B, but here the frame is less ornate. A Chippendale mirror in carved and gilt-wood after the Chinese taste is shown at C. It is nearly five feet in height, and has a pagoda top with Chinese figure, and a swan motif at the base.

Towards the end of the century, frames in the so-called classic style with arched cresting, sides of balustrading, and decorative motifs such as urns and acanthus foliage, appeared in response to the influence of the Adam brothers. Pier-glasses reaching to the frieze of a room are illustrated in their book.[2] A typical Adam mirror is shown in Plate 10(D), with urn motif, a popular decorative feature in the Adam taste.

Regency or Empire styles followed in the nineteenth century. The tendency for the height to be greater in proportion to the width was much less evident, and, in the later Victorian period, the

[1] William Ince and Thomas Mayhew, *Universal System of Household Furniture*, 1763, Plate LXXX.
[2] Robert and James Adam, *The Works in Architecture*, 3 Vols, London 1778–1822.

height and width were almost the same — in other words, the pier-glass assumed the shape of the ordinary wall mirror.

The Regency style pier-glasses are without any great merit. In the main they are rather coarse, much too ornate, and of poor quality; the early individual craftsmanship had begun to give place to the mass-produced article of the factory. The heavy and elaborate crestings, sometimes of figures, were intended to have classic appeal, but the stucco frames in their metallic gilding, ornamented with flowers and garlands also in stucco work, failed to capture that rich quality that had characterized the gilt gesso pier-glass of the early eighteenth century.

CHIMNEY-GLASSES

Although pier-glasses probably accounted for about two-thirds of eighteenth-century looking glasses, chimney-glasses were popular articles in well-furnished houses. The chimney-glass was fixed between the shelf above the chimneypiece and the entablature, the cornice at the top of the wainscot. They were at first of horizontal shape, but as the century progressed they became squarer in design, and later tended to become vertical, more like a pier-glass.

Chimney-glasses at the beginning of the eighteenth century were usually in three pieces, stretching across the chimneypiece itself. Like the pier-glasses, they were designed to give the impression of spaciousness and depth to the room, by reflecting the windows and other appointments in it.

Some chimney-glasses had a picture above the mirror, which formed a sort of overmantel. The mirror itself was usually in three separate pieces, the central piece being about twice the length of the two end pieces. The picture extended over all three mirrors; the whole being contained in a single frame. An excellent example of chimney-glasses following this style is shown in Plate 11(A). The frame in this example is walnut and gilt, the subject of the picture being after Hondekoeter.

In some cases these mirrors were painted by artists well known at the time; for example, a notice in *The Daily Courant* of December 6, 1771, spoke of 'Noble large Looking Glasses, finely painted with Flowers and Ornaments by Van Zoon'. Van Zoon had a reputation towards the end of the seventeenth century for his paintings of flowers. Another Dutch artist who painted flowers on mirror-glass was Van Huysum. Some chimney-glasses had landscape pictures, and sporting scenes or paintings in Chinese style. An occasional chimney-glass is found with a panel in needlework in place of the picture.

The frames of chimney-glasses followed much the same style as those used for the pier-glasses; gilt gesso styles were followed by frames in various woods such as walnut and laburnum, and in scrolled gilt wood, which, in their turn gave place to classic styles dictated by the fashions set by the Adam brothers.

Soon after the formation of the British Cast Plate Glass Company in 1773, mirrors began to be made not only larger, but in one piece. Nevertheless, there was still keen competition from France, and some of the larger mirrors designed by Robert Adam were imported from that country. Sheraton[1] records that nearly half the demands for mirrors in this country were supplied by France.

Repton[2] maintained that the correct use of mirrors with respect to light and cheerfulness of rooms was achieved during the early nineteenth century by large mirrors placed to produce 'elegant deception — a looking-glass over the chimney will increase the light and double the landscape in the country'.

For the town house, however, where lighting for evening receptions had to be taken into account, Repton preferred mirrors on the pier-walls; 'the light from the lustres and girandoles will be increased by mirrors so placed'.

IRISH MIRRORS

The classic styles of Robert Adam led to oval mirrors with gilt frames, with acanthus leaves as cresting and at the base. It was about this time (1780–90) that the Irish glasshouses were beginning to produce mirrors, notably in Dublin and the south of Ireland. They were also oval in shape, with frames made up of facets of coloured glass; dark blue, green and opaque white were some of the colours used.

Some of the rarer specimens of oval mirrors are found with frames having two rows of facets. A specimen in the National Museum, Dublin, has the outer row of clear glass, and the inner of alternate pieces of dark blue and opaque white with gold flutes. In some cases, there is a small chandelier suspended in front of the mirror, such as that shown in Plate 11(B). This specimen, about four feet in height, has the double row of facets.

Other Irish specimens have a scroll base, such as that shown in Plate 11(C). This example, about two feet six inches in height, also has the double border, one of clear facets and the other of blue

[1] Thomas Sheraton, *Cabinet Dictionary*, London 1803.
[2] Humphry Repton, *Fragments on the Theory and Practise of Landscape Gardening*, 1816, p. 150.

13. DRINKING GLASSES, 19TH CENTURY

A: Liqueur glass with acid-embossed decoration; last quarter of the 19th century. B: Glassware taken from the catalogue of the Great Exhibition. C: Wineglass; second half of the 19th century. D: Wineglass in imitation of earlier style; late 19th century. E: Tumbler with flute decoration; late 19th century. F: Wineglass with ruby tinted bowl; second half of the 19th century.

14. ENGRAVED GLASSES

A: Group of drinking glasses engraved with hops and barley and growing vine motifs. (*Messrs Arthur Churchill.*) B: Coronation glass of George I with moulded sceptres and inscribed 'G. R.' (*Mr Cecil Davis*). C: Glass commemorating the coronation of George II. D: George III Coronation Glass bearing the Royal Arms and inscription 'G III R'. E: Scent-bottle by Apsley Pellatt with bust of William IV. F: Loving Cup commemorating the coronation of H. M. Queen Elizabeth II. (*Messrs Stevens & Williams Ltd.*)

facets alternating, with white opaque with gilt flutes. Both these mirrors (11, B and C) may be dated about 1780.

CONVEX MIRRORS

There has already been reference to the convex mirrors made by the glassmakers of Nuremberg.[1] It was not until the end of the eighteenth century, however, that the convex mirror was manufactured in this country. Sheraton described the new type of looking glass[2]: 'As an article in furniture, a mirror is a circular convex glass in a gilt frame, silvered on the concave side, by which the reflection of the rays of light are produced. The properties of such mirrors consist in their collecting the reflected rays into a point, by which the perspective of the room in which they are suspended presents itself in the surface of the mirror, and produces an agreeable effect. On this account, as well as for the convenience of holding lights, they are now become universally in fashion and are considered both as a useful and ornamental piece of furniture.'

Convex mirrors were usually given frames of carved wood and were ornamented in gilt often with a single row of small gilt balls set in a channel in the frame. There was usually an ancanthus leaf or laurel leaf cresting, but in some cases the cresting was of a figure subject, such as an eagle, a sea-horse or more complex designs.

As two walls of a room in the Regency period were already occupied by mirrors, that is the pier wall and the facing chimney wall, the circular concave mirrors usually occupied a position on an end wall, which enabled them to reflect the entire contents of the room.

[1] See p. 73.   [2] Thomas Sheraton, *Cabinet Dictionary. op. cit.*

CHAPTER EIGHT

Drinking Glasses

THERE has been an ever-increasing interest in the collecting of old drinking glasses since Hartshorne[1] published his classification of them half-a-century ago. During the last twenty years or so, many books have appeared on the subject, and as the classification becomes more accurate and comprehensive, the circle of collectors has widened from what was at first an exclusive English interest to a fascinating pursuit covering two hemispheres.

The period of interest to the majority of collectors is the eighteenth century. This is the happy hunting ground from which nine-tenths of the average collections will have been selected. It was the period when the English glass-maker established for himself a reputation that was the envy of the civilized world. But the English triumph was short-lived. By the time the Irish glasshouses closed their doors in the early part of the nineteenth century, the best period of English glass-making had long been passed.

Although the first half of the eighteenth century is regarded as the classic period, English glass-making sprang into prominence late in the seventeenth century, mainly due to the foresight of a group of business men, the Glass Sellers' Company, which had received a renewed charter in 1664. Their business was to sell glass, obtained either from the home manufacturers or imported from abroad. The main supply came from Venice, but from documents which still exist[2] it is evident that the Glass Sellers' Company was, for many reasons, dissatisfied with the quality. Indeed, in 1671 there was a strong warning to the Venetian manufacturers that future supplies would be sought in the home market.

Experiments had already been conducted in this country some years before with the object of improving the quality of the home product, but it is evident that by 1671 the Glass Sellers were firmly determined to make their glass where they made their sales. In 1674 they became associated with George Ravenscroft, an English gentleman with a leaning towards science, and who had been interested in the Venetian trade. He had been at work on the problem at a glasshouse in the Savoy, London. The association met with

[1] A. Hartshorne, *Old English Glasses*, London, 1897.
[2] Sloane MS. 857, *Papers relating to Glass-Sellers*. Now in the British Museum.

quick success, and in 1676 a new medium, known as glass-of-lead, had been established commercially. The Glass Sellers were able to advertise their 'new flint glasses', and to distinguish them by a 'Seal or Mark' in the form of a raven's head — a compliment to Ravenscroft for his achievement. Some of these sealed glasses still exist.

The new glass-of-lead was immediately popular. It was adopted in glasshouses all over the country, at centres as widely dispersed as Bristol, Stourbridge, Liverpool, Yarmouth and the Isle of Wight; before the end of the century no less than twenty-seven glasshouses were producing it.

Ravenscroft's glass-of-lead was quite different from anything that had been produced before. Because of the high proportion of lead it contained — about one-third by weight — it had remarkable properties of light dispersion. When cut, it surpassed the diamond in its properties of reflection and refraction, a property, strangely enough, that was not fully exploited for a full century later. A new technique had to be learned by the glass-maker for its manipulation — its working properties were quite different from the glass used by either the Bohemian or Venetian glass-makers — but by the end of the century, he had succeeded in blending his medium with English ideas of form into a fascinating range of drinking vessels. These are known by collectors today as baluster glasses, and mark the beginnings of a purely English style. They are important to collectors because it is the earliest group of glasses from which a series can be formed.

The character of the glasses changed many times throughout the century due to political and foreign influences, but in the main they can be divided into clearly defined groups, based very much on the formation of their stems. The stem was a feature that varied most during the century, the bowl and the foot showing by comparison only slight modifications. The following[1] is the general classification adopted today by collectors:

Baluster stemmed glasses	1682–1715
Silesian stemmed glasses	1715–1750
Balustroid stemmed glasses	1700–1745
Light Newcastle glasses	1730–1780
Plain stemmed glasses	1720–1800
Air-twist stemmed glasses	1730–1760
Incised-twist stemmed glasses	1750–1765
Opaque-twist stemmed glasses	1745–1780
Mixed and coloured twist stemmed glasses	1760–1780
Cut glasses	1740–1800

[1] E. M. Elville, *English Tableglass*, London, 1951, p. 80.

It will be seen from the given table that there is a certain amount of overlapping of dates. No distinct line can be drawn in this respect; glasses made in London, for example, had long ceased to be fashionable when similar styles were still popular in provincial centres. On the other hand, there was always a demand for certain styles of glasses while others were being developed. A general line of development, however, can be traced from the baluster period at the end of the seventeenth century to the cut-glass period at the end of the eighteenth century, as follows: balusters — air twists — opaque twists — cut glasses.

BALUSTER STEMMED GLASSES

In the years immediately following Ravenscroft's invention, the glass-maker had not gained sufficient confidence in himself to express his own individuality, and the early form still showed Venetian influence; the glass shown in Plate 12(A), with inverted baluster stem is typical of the period. This motif was the English version of the Venetian urn-shaped stem, and the true baluster was copied directly from the Venetian glasses; indeed, it was a motif in Renaissance architecture.

These simple motifs, however, were very quickly elaborated into numerous other stem styles. The glass-maker borrowed from architectural ornament, adopted Continental ideas which he reproduced with a strong native flavour, and was inspired by simple naturalistic motifs. He combined and modified them into numerous complicated forms which almost defy description, and much of the early simplicity and grace was lost.

Some of the devices employed were in themselves simple, such as a ball, a drop, an acorn or a mushroom, and up to 1715 knops of these forms characterized the stem formation, but after that period the knops themselves became more complicated, such as the Silesian stems (1715), multiple knops (1720) and annulated or triple-ring knops (1725).

Towards the end of the first quarter of the century, the stem became longer at the expense of the bowl, and more complicated knopping followed. The general form was much lighter, however, than the early balusters, and the variation infinitely greater. These stems, which were the natural evolutionary development of the earlier styles, persisted up to the middle of the century. They are known to collectors as balustroids, and strictly speaking include such glasses as the light Newcastle glasses, which were the specialized products of one or two provincial factories.

All the earlier motifs were employed, but the distinguishing feature of at least half the glasses was the inverted baluster. It was not so definite in form as in the early balusters, but an adaptation of it appeared either alone or in combination with other knops. Towards the middle of the century, knopping was much less in evidence, and many balustroid glasses are found in which a single knop is the only distinguishing feature of the stem.

AIR-TWIST STEMMED GLASSES

Through the balustroid period to the eighteenth century's end, there was a demand for glasses with plain stems. It is not unreasonable to assume that they represented what might be termed the utility glasses of the period for use in the taverns and cottages. They were the cheapest form of drinking glassware, because they were made by the easiest method, that is, the bowl and stem were made in one piece by being drawn from a blob of hot glass; the foot was afterwards attached by a separate operation. They were known as 'drawn shanks', but today are referred to as two-piece glasses.

Because they were intended to be cheap, they were plain; there was no knopping of the stem or applied embellishments such as engraving or cutting. The only relief from bareness was the use of a 'tear' in the upper part of the stem. This was formed when the glass was being made, by denting the hot blob of glass with a blunt tool, and covering it with a second layer of glass. The entrapped air expanded with the heat, and while the glass was being drawn, became elongated into a spherical bubble or almost to thread formation.

It is evident that the tear formations inspired the air-twist style of decoration. The simple tear quickly gave place to a multiplicity of smaller drawn threads, and they in their turn were elaborated into a great variety of fascinating lace-like patterns in single spiral form and multiple combination.

The glass-maker employed all his ingenuity and skill in the making of air-twist glasses. He learned to make them by the stuck shank method, that is, the glass was made in three separate pieces — bowl, stem, and foot — which enabled a greater variety of bowl form to be employed, and also allowed the use of knops to elaborate the stem. Indeed, it was when the glass-maker mastered the technique of making air-twist stems with knops that the real beauty of this form of decoration was displayed. A typical three-piece specimen is shown in Plate 12(B).

The air-twist stem can be regarded as a purely English development; it is the most aesthetically effective of all forms of glass adornment, for it displays the beauty of the medium, its sparkle and inherent brilliance, without the necessity of applied embellishments such as cutting and engraving.

OPAQUE-TWIST STEMMED GLASSES

Fashions in glass changed quickly in the eighteenth century. This is apparent from the many and varied styles of glasses that remain as evidence, and from the notices appearing in the newspapers and journals of the period. There were well over a score of descriptions from 'Curious cut glass' in 1727 to 'the present fashion' in 1785.

It is, however, difficult to trace the reason for the change in fashion from the elegant air-twist stemmed glasses to those in which the drawn threads were replaced by opaque white glass, or, as it was then termed, enamel. This occurred about the middle of the century, when attempts were being made at several centres in this country to reproduce Continental porcelain.[1] The principle of making glasses with opaque-twist stems has already been described.[2]

At first only simple twists were attempted in which a few opaque threads were spaced evenly in the mould to give a single spiral in the stem. With the wide experience of air-twist stems behind him, however, the glass-maker quickly mastered the new technique, and the simple spirals became elaborated into a countless variety of fascinating lace-like patterns. For example, when a circle of canes was placed eccentrically in the core of the mould, on stretching and twisting, it became a spiral gauze, appearing something like a corkscrew; two, three, and even four of these gauzes may be found combined together in one stem.

The glass-maker increased his range of patterns when he found that the process of picking up the canes of opaque glass from the mould could be repeated, resulting in a double series of canes in one formation. This double series soon became the more popular variety, three glasses in every four with opaque-twist stems consisting of this type. A typical glass of this series is shown in Plate 12(c).

Opaque-twist stems were popular until 1777, in which year enamel glass, as the opaque variety was termed, was considered of sufficient importance to tax. Manufacture of opaque stems then virtually ceased, and cut-glass stems, which had waged an unequal price war with the opaque-twist variety since 1745, enjoyed a free market.

[1] See p. 56.   [2] See p. 54.

CUT-STEMMED GLASSES

Cut stems had appeared before 1777, but they were unable to compete then in price with the opaque-twist stemmed glasses. The cutter had been forced to provide as little cutting as possible and confined his attention mainly to the stems. The diamonds with which the stems were decorated, such as the specimen shown in Plate 12(D), were purposely made longer vertically than they were across in order to save time, and therefore cost, in the cutting operation.[1]

After 1777, however, the cutter had more scope, and extended his attention to the bowls and the feet. The diamonds also became more equilateral towards the end of the century, and were made smaller to enhance reflection, and, therefore, the sparkle of the glass.

Bowls were first cut at the base, in a form of cresting to the stems. Diamond and hexagon motifs extended up from the top of the stem to the underside of the bowl. Later the cutting extended almost to the top of the bowl, sometimes entirely of diamond motifs, or of fluting.

The feet of the cut glasses were also decorated by the cutter in broad flutes radiating from the stem and corresponding scallop border to the rim of the foot.

SPECIAL GLASSES

The foregoing is a description of the more ordinary glasses as they developed during the eighteenth century. There was, of course, an overlapping of styles. For example, it had been customary to employ what was known as a 'folded foot' up to the middle of the eighteenth century when the Glass Excise Act (1745–6) enforced its abandonment. The folded foot was made by folding the rim of the foot under the base, forming a double layer of glass on which the vessel stood; the folded rim varied from a quarter of an inch up to more than half an inch on some of the larger glasses, such as the balusters.

Although the fold was abandoned after the Excise Act of 1745–6 because of the necessity to economize on the material, a glass with this feature is sometimes found on specimens of later styles. Such a glass is therefore rare, and is an interesting one to add to a collection. Much the same applies to knopping, which was a common feature before the Glass Excise Act. A knopped glass of the second half of the eighteenth century is therefore worthy of consideration.

[1] E. M. Elville, *English and Irish Cut Glass*, p. 24 *et seq.*

Other interesting glasses from the eighteenth century are those developed for special drinks such as rum, posset, caudle, syllabub, mead and ratafia. A description of them follows.

THE RUMMER

Although it is generally understood that the capacious goblet of general utility known as the rummer assumed the form with which we are familiar today during the second half of the eighteenth century, there is no doubt that it was known long before that period. The name 'rummer' occurs in the seventeenth century in connection with tavern names; a 'Rummer Tavern' was known at Charing Cross in 1682 and there was one at Bristol a few years later.

It is significant that these taverns were at ports, from which it might be assumed that the rummer had some connection with the vessels that plied between this country and the English colonies in Jamaica and America from which was imported a form of rum. Rum did not come into use in its modern form until bonding became legal in 1742, but a rum made by distilling sugar-cane had then been known in England for some time.

An explanation for the origin of the term rummer must be sought in some other direction, however, for in the seventeenth century 'a rummer of Rhenish' was a well-used expression. It is evident, moreover, that even in those early days the rummer had begun to establish for itself a reputation of general utility. Merret[1] speaks of 'the Romer for Rheinish wine, for Sack, Claret, Beer'. Indeed, its generous capacity may have recommended its use for water, assuming, of course, that there was an occasional necessity in those hard-drinking days for so humble a beverage.

The explanation generally accepted today, is that the word rummer is a corruption of the German *roemer*, and that it had no significance in its conception with the spirit rum. The roemer was typically a German glass used for the Rhine wines, and the custom of using such glasses was adopted with the introduction to this country of the wines of the Rhine and the Moselle.

There is no mention of the rummer in the English newspaper notices until 1751, and only after 1772 do they become at all common. There is no doubt that it did not become a fashionable glass until it had evolved into something like its now familiar form. This was a slow process. The German form was absorbed and reproduced with such strong native flavour that the original *roemer* and the nineteenth-century rummer have no points in common.

[1] C. Merret, *The Art of Glass*, 1662, pp. 225–6.

Thorpe[1] has traced its evolution through a number of stages, beginning with the English version of the German *roemer* made by George Ravenscroft and given his seal of the raven's head. A specimen at the Victoria and Albert Museum has a cup-shaped bowl, ribbed vertically with a hollow, bucket-shaped stem with prunts, and vermicular collar; the foot is of the pedestal type, radially ribbed. This glass would have been made during the period of the Savoy and Henley glass houses, between 1676 and 1678.

After a period of three or four years, the style had become slightly modified. The bowl was now changed to a wide, incurved style with gadrooned base, the stem hollow with prunts, and the foot plain, and the tendency to follow this style was maintained until the end of the seventeenth century. About 1690 the hollow bucket stem was replaced by a solid knopped one, a popular motif being the ordinary baluster. The folded foot became a feature about 1700.

The German ancestry of the rummer was now no longer in evidence. The German form had followed a proportionate balance between bowl, stem and foot; the English version by comparison always gives the impression of being unsymmetrical, the bowl being too large for the insignificant stem and foot.

From 1700 onwards the progress to the style which was still popular a century later is not easy to follow. New styles were introduced in response to the influence of the Adam brothers, and the bowls of these glasses were often decorated by engraving in simple border styles. Commemorative engraving appeared on some glasses, most bowl forms being popular with the engraver with the exception of the round funnel style.

Such glasses were still fashionable at the time of the Great Exhibition in 1851. An example of the style at that time is shown in Plate 12(E). The usual form was a generous bowl on a short stem, sometimes embellished with simple knops, mounted on a plain spreading foot. The bowl forms were numerous; ovoid, bucket-shaped, round funnel, ogee and double ogee, were some of the more popular forms. A square-cut base, which could be terraced or ridged, was also fashionable. These styles were in vogue up to the end of the last century.

POSSET AND CAUDLE GLASSES

Posset was a drink made of curdled milk with ale or wine, to which were added fine bread-crumbs. It was used on social and convivial

---

[1] W. A. Thorpe, *History of English and Irish Glass, op. cit.*, p. 327.

occasions, much the same as caudle, a curious hot drink prepared from mulled wine or ale, thickened with bread and sugar, and seasoned with various spices.

Posset and caudle cups were similar in form, the general type being a squat straight- or round-sided vessel with cover, and provided with one or two spouts and a handle. Indeed, some of them had the appearance of the modern tea-pot. It is quite possible, moreover, that the tea-pot of today is a development of the early posset and caudle pots, as it is known that when tea-drinking was first introduced in this country, the posset and caudle pots were called into service. Tea itself was scarce and expensive, and drunk only once a fortnight by well-to-do City tradesmen and families, but eventually tea must have superseded posset and caudle for fashionable afternoon gatherings.

MEAD GLASSES

Mead was an old-world drink, dating from the time of our Saxon ancestors, and was a potent brew prepared from honey and seasoned with herbs. It was said to have been 'woundily strong' and needed only a small glass. It was an exceedingly popular drink in the seventeenth and eighteenth centuries and, indeed, mead drinking was a custom that lingered in some country districts until the nineteenth century. There have been revivals among mead enthusiasts even in recent times. Many varieties of mead were known such as Sack Mead, Walnut Mead, Cowslip Mead, Spiced Mead and Small Mead, the varieties taking their names from the character of the main seasoning ingredients.

The particular type of glass used for mead has, like the champagne glass, always been a controversial matter. Tradition claims that mead glasses were of low or tumbler form. There is no doubt that they must have been easy glasses to manufacture, and therefore of some simple design, for, owing to the great popularity of mead, they would have been required in quantity. It is, of course, likely that any small bowl, capable of being used as a drinking glass, would be called into service.

Some writers claim, however, that, like many other drinks in the eighteenth century, mead had its special glasses, and that the most popular style was a bowl, often incurved and with lip finish, usually about three inches in height, or a low, tumbler-shaped vessel, waisted in the middle and with a kick bottom, that is, indented at the base similar to a modern champagne bottle. Bowls for mead were, of course, advertised during the eighteenth century.

SYLLABUB GLASSES

Much in the same category as the mead glasses were those used for syllabub. This was an insipid, rather nauseous drink, judged by modern standards, but popular and well-appreciated in the seventeenth and eighteenth centuries. It was prepared from cream fresh from the cow, whipped to a froth, and sack, seasoned with ratafia, and spices such as cinnamon. The final feature of the preparation was that of 'stroking' it at the cow's side.

Special glasses were used for syllabub, but there is no doubt that they changed considerably in form during the period in which they were advertised, roughly one hundred years. The earlier practice was to drink syllabub like posset through the spout of a glass or earthenware vessel with two handles but there is no doubt that punch bowls and ladles with ordinary wineglasses were also employed.

There was an early reference to 'Syllabub glasses' in 1677 in connection with George Ravenscroft, and these can no doubt be identified with the sealed posset glasses of that period. It would seem that from the notices appearing in the newspapers about the mid-eighteenth century, that there was a difference between the glasses used for the two beverages, for, from 1731 to 1775, syllabub glasses are advertised frequently by themselves. The alternative name 'whips', short for whipt-syllabub, also appears. It is most probable that there was a gradual transition from the posset glass to the jelly glass, first the spout and then the handles being dispensed with. There are some late seventeenth-century glasses extant shaped very much like the early posset glasses, but with no spout and only one handle.

Syllabub and jelly glasses after 1770 were identified together in the same advertisements: 'Jelly and Syllabub Glasses'. Buckley[1] points out that the idea that the two glasses were practically identical is shown by specimens of jelly glasses engraved with the letter S, as though to distinguish them from jelly glasses of similar shape.

RATAFIA GLASSES

The eighteenth-century equivalent of the modern cocktail and liqueur were the cordials, spirituous drinks prepared from the juice and kernels of fruits such as apricots, cherries and peaches, and from the peel of the citron, orange and lemon. Special glasses were devised for their consumption.

A fashionable cordial was ratafia, a drink which was introduced

[1] F. Buckley, *History of Old English Glass, op. cit.*, p, 115.

about the end of the seventeenth century; it was flavoured with the kernels of almonds, peach or cherries. It had its own special glass, usually of slender flute form; a typical specimen is shown in Plate 12(F) with opaque-twist stem of the 1750–60 period. Some are found with the bowl engraved with floral border or with the bowl moulded at the base with light flutes, such as in this specimen.

COIN AND DICE GLASSES

The custom of enclosing a coin in the hollow stem of a drinking glass would appear to have originated in Murano. Glasses of this type were presented to distinguished persons visiting the island. There is a specimen in the British Museum of a Venetian coin glass in which is enclosed a half sequin of Francesco Molino, who was Doge in 1647.

The fashion of enclosing a coin in the stem was probably introduced into this country about the time of Charles II, for several specimens are known which contain coins of the King. The character of some of these glasses indicate that they were made during that period. It is, of course, not necessarily the case that the date of the coin is that of the glass in which it is enclosed. For example, another coin glass in the British Museum contains a threepenny piece of 1679, but the glass is obviously of a very much later period, probably mid-eighteenth century.

It is claimed by Francis[1] 'that all the glasses between 1715 and 1750 which contain Charles II coins are as definitely Jacobite as if they bore the portrait of Prince Charles himself, and that glasses containing coins of William III, Anne, George I and George II, of the same period, are as much anti-Jacobite as are the glasses engraved '*To the Immortal Memory of King William*'.

There are examples of the Queen Anne period extant, some with a fourpenny piece of 1710 in the stem. A typical style is a wine with bell bowl and folded foot, and hollow knopped and prunted stem.

Enclosed coins are not confined to drinking glasses. Tankards are known with coins of George II, and jugs with coins enclosed in the base have always enjoyed a certain amount of popularity. They were especially in demand during the reign of Victoria, on the occasion of the Great Exhibition and the Jubilee in 1887.

Coin glasses were re-introduced for the coronation of Her Majesty Queen Elizabeth II, and goblets and other drinking vessels with a 1953 coin enclosed in the hollow stem were popular items designed to celebrate the occasion.

[1] G. Francis, *Old English Drinking Glasses*, London 1926, p. 206.

Although coin glasses were in favour in this country over a long period, it is doubtful whether dice glasses were ever popular. They were, however, known on the Continent. The Germanisches Museum at Nuremberg has fluted Bohemian tumblers, three and a half inches in height, which contain three ivory dice in the bottom. It is assumed that the 'call' for drinks was decided by the throw of the dice.

NINETEENTH-CENTURY DRINKING GLASSES

Although the period of interest to the majority of collectors of drinking glasses is the eighteenth century, there are many who are turning their attention to glasses of the nineteenth. Little has been written as yet on development of glasses from the year 1800 onwards, yet it was one of the most important periods in the history of tableglass. Its advent saw cut decoration at the height of its popularity; by the close of the century it had gone almost completely out of fashion. The general form and shape, which at the beginning of the century had been much the same as those prevailing at the close of the eighteenth, changed many times during the Victorian era, only to emerge at the end of the century in a condition of still greater uncertainty. It was a period when the form and style, not only of drinking glasses, but of every variety and kind of glass, were in the melting pot in more senses than one.

There were many influences at work to account for the transition in form: the industrial revolution early in the century, the debasement of the cut article, the innovation of blown-moulded and pressed glass, the repeal of the Glass Excise Act in 1845, the effect of censure by such critics of art as John Ruskin and William Morris, and the influence of glass craftsmen and artists such as Apsley Pellatt, Harry Powell and John Northwood. The history of tableglass during the period has been discussed at length in an earlier book.[1]

At the time of the Great Exhibition, it is evident that the heavier modes that had developed following the advent of machinery had largely begun to be discarded, and vessels with light and refined proportions more suited to the delicate and fragile nature of the material were now becoming more fashionable. A group of glasses from the period taken from the Catalogue of the Great Exhibition is shown in Plate 13(B).

It was about this period too that William Morris commissioned Phillip Webb, the architect, to design some tableglass employing

[1] E. M. Elville, *English and Irish Cut Glass, op. cit.,* pp. 71–83.

simple outlines. Morris, whose ideas combined the qualities of utility with those of craftsmanship, favoured the use of the inherent qualities of the material to enhance its effect, and dispensed with applied decoration such as cutting and engraving.

The Morris school of thought permitted the use of coloured and tinted glass, and shortly after the Exhibition of 1851 coloured drinking glasses became the vogue. Only two manufacturers had shown them at the Exhibition, but with the blessing of the critics the fashion quickly grew. Ruby, bright green, emerald green, light peacock-green, dark purple and canary-yellow were the more usual colours for wineglasses. A typical glass of the period, with ruby-tinted bowl, is shown in Plate 13(F).

Another popular innovation by the Stourbridge manufacturers shortly after the mid-century was 'old gold' threaded glass, for which a process was employed of closely winding threads of delicately tinted glass over colourless or pale ruby tableware. A champagne glass decorated in this manner was accorded a prize in a competition held by the Society of Arts in 1869.

On the other hand, there is no doubt concerning the influence of the Morris school of thought, for during the last quarter of the century, glasses made their appearance marked by their simple form and lightness of decoration, but it cannot be claimed by any stretch of the imagination that they were inspired.

There was also a rather vague effort to capture the classical outline of the early balusters, such as in the specimens shown in Plate 13(C and D), but the temptation to add a few simple cut motifs was irresistible, and flutes were employed on the lower half of the bowl in an attempt to add to the appeal. This effort was even extended to the common tumblers of the period, such as shown in Plate 13(E).

Decoration of glasses during the last quarter of the nineteenth and the beginning of the twentieth centuries was often applied by acid embossing (Plate 13, A), that is, the motif was etched on the surface of the glass by the action of hydrofluoric acid. Acid-embossed glasses of the late nineteenth century are now scarce, and are already 'priced' in the antique shops.

CHAPTER NINE

Engraved Commemorative Glasses

DURING the last few years, a handful of talented artists in various parts of the world have revived the art of glass engraving. They have thrown in sharp focus the fact that engraving is the most expressive and appropriate of all applied forms of glass decoration.

Engraving on glass has been practised since early Christian times. Pliny described it in the first century A.D. in his book on Natural History. Italian craftsmen employed the process for the carving of rock crystal during the Renaissance, and, at the beginning of the seventeenth century, Caspar Lehmann revived its application to glass at Prague. Dutch and German craftsmen became highly proficient in the art of glass engraving during the seventeenth century, and shortly afterwards it was adopted in this country.

There are two styles of glass engraving, one in which a small metal wheel, carried in a lathe and fed with an abrasive material, is used to grind away the glass surface; the other in which a diamond or a sharp steel point is used to scratch a design upon the glass. During the eighteenth century, however, the method of glass engraving in this country was almost entirely with the wheel.

The process is a simple one and has varied little in principle since Roman times. The essential component is a copper wheel rotated in a lathe operated by a foot treadle. An abrasive mixture of oil with emery or carborundum powder is smeared upon the edge of the wheel, and the glass brought into contact with it, the slightest touch being sufficient to grind a dull, greyish-white mark upon the glass. The wheels used are interchangeable and of great variety, the larger ones being about four inches in diameter, up to a quarter of an inch in thickness, and the smallest not much larger than a pin's head. The edges are bevelled in various ways, and are prepared by the craftsman himself; much of his skill depends on their preparation and selection.

Unless the engraver is an exceptional craftsman, it is customary to mark out the design upon the glass with a mixture of gum and chalk. The heavier portions of the design are then roughed out, a coarse grain of emery and a wide wheel with a flat edge being used

95

for this purpose. As the design develops, the wheels are changed, and a finer grade of emery used to add the detailed work in the design. In the case of a decoration requiring different shading effects, wheels of lead, wood, cork or rubber are employed to give varying degrees of polish to the engraved surfaces.

Glass engraving is the most expressive of all applied methods of decorating glassware, and calls for very patient and skilful work on the part of the craftsman. Not only does his subject have to be depicted with good delineation, but much of the beauty of the work depends on his decision as to the depth of the engraved lines, and as to which parts of the design require to be left dull or to be polished. His difficulties are increased by the fact that he is unable to follow with his eye the progress of the work in hand, for not only has he to press the glass against the *underside* of the wheel, but that part of the surface on which he is working remains covered by the abrasive medium.

Considerable time, in some instances months, is necessary to produce a single specimen with this type of decoration, and many are works of art in the true sense of the word. The process has a wide scope: a design may vary from a simple sprig of leaves, for example, superficially engraved on the glass surface, to deeply carved figure subjects such as those of the Portland Vase.

Wheel engraving in this country followed much the same development as glass cutting. There is no positive evidence that it was practised to any extent before the beginning of the eighteenth century. No doubt the silversmiths and gem engravers occasionally applied their talents to glass objects, but in the main, wheel engraving as a craft can be regarded as beginning about the end of the first quarter of the eighteenth century, when certain events occurred which greatly influenced its development.

After the Treaty of Utrecht in 1713, engraved and cut glass was imported into western Europe on a large scale. It was then not only possible for merchants from Bohemia and other glass-making centres to export their wares westwards to such countries as Holland, with whom this country had a close business relationship, but for engravers and cutters of glass to exploit their knowledge of the craft in other countries.

Another important influence on English engraving was the accession in 1714 of George of Hanover to the English Throne. This event was responsible for the importation of many German customs and fashions, of which wheel engraving was one; moreover, facilities for the infiltration of German craftsmen were undoubtedly made easier after 1714. Yet, in spite of the stimulating influence of the Continental craftsmen, the English style that eventually emerged was markedly different from that of the Dutch and German schools. It would appear that the foreign influence lay only in the adoption of the idea, and not in its expression. English glassmakers at this period had unbounded confidence in themselves and in their medium; they preferred to maintain their own individuality, and to adopt new techniques to their own style. In this manner both Venetian and Continental styles were absorbed and reproduced with a strong native flavour.

But because of this conservatism of English taste, there was never any attempt at the elaborate design which marked the efforts of the Continental craftsmen. This may have been due, of course, to a lack of artistic talent in this style of work, for native engraving at its best appears amateurish; it lacks draughtsmanship, and never seriously approaches the artistic merit attained abroad. It was the work of skilled craftsmen rather than of talented artists.

Flowered Glasses

The early style of native engraving expressed itself in what may be termed the utility glassware of the period, in conventional borders of scroll work, formal flowers, birds and insects, described at the time by the term 'flowered' glasses. The term was first used in 1742 by Jerom Johnson in the *Daily Advertiser* of December 21: 'At the entire Glass Shop, the corner of St Martin's Lane — all cut and scalloped and flowered Glasses, shall always be sold cheapest by the maker, Jerom Johnson'.

Johnson was one of the pioneers of English decorative glass. He practised between the years 1739 and 1761, and was the first Englishman to show that wheel decoration could be applied to glass without foreign assistance. In most of his advertisements he described himself variously as the 'workman', the 'inventor' or the 'maker', and because of this, claimed that he could sell cheaper than any other engraver and cutter. He advertised almost every glass article, from a simple wineglass to 'the most magnificent lustre that ever was made in England'.

Johnson chose designs that expressed the flourish demanded by the rococo appeal; his flowered glasses were an appropriate subscription to a taste that at the time was sweeping Europe, but he chose simple emblems that could be easily appreciated by his public to interpret it. The roses, daffodils, hops and barley, carnations, honeysuckle, and the grapes and vine leaves were in themselves

G

sufficient to express the rococo fashion, but he freely employed curling leaves and slender twining tendrils to emphasize it.

Examples of what must have been fashionable engraved glasses during Johnson's time are shown in the group in Plate 14(A). They give variations of two of the most popular of all eighteenth-century emblems on drinking glasses, hops and barley and the growing vine.

Francis[1] describes the various positions in which the fancy or art of the engraver placed simple ears of barley and hop blossoms. The normal type of ale glass on which the motif is found was given two simple ears of barley in saltire, namely, with the stalks crossed diagonally, and having a single leaf on each stalk on one side of the glass, with a single hop blossom dependent from tendrils bearing two leaves on the reverse side. Ten variations of this motif are given by Francis.

The growing vine, consisting of bunches of grapes and vine leaves, was another extremely popular form of decoration; indeed, it is still used today by engravers.

The custom of specializing glasses grew during the eighteenth century, and the engraved emblems were appropriate to the beverage for which the glass was intended; hops and barley for ale and beer glasses, the growing vine for wineglasses, and apple trees for cider-glasses were some of the popular motifs.

Examples of engraving so far considered have been of a definite decorative character, intended to enhance the vessel by improving its appearance and appeal, or perhaps to give it a little deeper significance when the engraved emblems on a glass bore some relationship with the beverage it was expected to contain.

CORONATION GLASSES

There is another much more important group of glasses, however, of which the engraving records an event, a sentiment or toast, political or social, that at the time was considered of importance. They are today termed commemorative glasses. For over two thousand years, it has been customary to record important events on glass. Roman gladiators were given engraved trophies in glass commemorating their feats and victories; excellent examples can be seen in museums throughout Italy. Later Venetian armorial glasses in coloured enamels were emulated by Bohemian and Dutch craftsmen who specialized in the technique of engraving with either the wheel or the diamond point.

Commemorative engraving in this country, however, cannot be

[1] Grant Francis, *Old English Drinking Glasses, op. cit.*

said to have commenced much before the Restoration, and a glass engraved to celebrate the coronation of Charles II in 1660 is probably the first of what might be termed coronation glasses. This glass, termed the Exeter Flute, now in the Royal Albert Museum, Exeter, is considered by authorities to have been made in London for the Coronation of Charles II in 1660. Although the style, known as *façon de Venice*, shows strong Continental influence, the glass was probably made by Italian craftsmen then in this country, and engraved by a Dutch artist. The decoration is diamond-point work showing a bust of Charles II in a medallion, and the stump of an oak tree. The inscription round the rim is 'God Bless King Charles the Second'.

It was shortly after the Restoration that glass manufacture in this country became more generally applied. Enormous impetus was due to the discovery in 1676 of George Ravenscroft's glass-of-lead, and in the early years of the eighteenth century form and style developed rapidly.

The accession in 1714 of George I, Elector of Hanover and a great grandson of James I, to the English Throne is well recorded in glassware. In spite of the fact that George I was almost unknown in this country, spoke little English, and openly preferred his native Hanover, the English nevertheless accepted him well. Indeed, so far as glassware is concerned, several Continental styles were adopted and became fashionable as a gesture to the new King.

Coronation drinking glasses must have been popular at the time, for several different styles are known. The more usual is that shown in Plate 14(B). The moulded Silesian stem was a fashion introduced into this country at the time of the accession, and some specimens, such as that illustrated, had sceptres or the letters G.R. moulded in relief on the four shoulders of the stem. Some rare examples have 'God Save King George' or 'God Save King G' impressed upon them.

The coronation of George II in 1727 is also recorded in glass. The specimen shown in Plate 14(C) is a beautiful example of the light baluster stem with twisted bubbles of air, a style then coming into fashion. These bubbles, in later specimens, were elaborated into the air-twist stem,[1] the most aesthetically effective of any kind of glass decoration.

The George II glass, because of the elegance and great brilliancy of the material, was at one time thought to have been manufactured on the Continent to the order of the English Court, but it is

[1] See p. 85.

now fairly certain that it was of Newcastle origin, although probably engraved by a foreign hand.

The glass shown in Plate 14(D) records the accession in 1760 of George III to the English Throne. It bears the Royal Arms and the inscription G.III.R., the work being partly in diamond point. The air-twist stem, which had its beginnings in the previous reign, had by then been fully developed to apply to glasses made in three pieces, bowl, stem and foot.

Nearly sixty years elapsed before the historian in glass was again called upon to record a coronation. Owing to the mental aberration of George III, his eldest son had been appointed Regent in 1811, and, in 1820 acceded to the Throne. The usual style of George IV coronation glass is the rummer, the robust and capacious goblet of general utility which became a fashionable shape towards the change of the century.[1] The generous ovoid or bucket-shaped bowls of the rummers allowed the engraver plenty of scope, and they were chosen for commemorating all important events of the period. Typical examples were the English 'Volunteer' glasses following the French Revolution in 1789, 'Sunderland Bridge' rummers depicting the opening of the new bridge at Sunderland in 1796, 'Nelson' glasses which showed portraits of the Admiral and the *Victory*, and 'Wellington' glasses commemorating Waterloo in 1815.

Barely a decade had passed before William, Duke of Clarence, and third son of George III, acceded to the Throne as William IV. The industrial revolution was then in full swing. The first application of steam power had occurred at Brettle Lane, Stourbridge, in 1807, and in a remarkably short space of time, power-driven cutting wheels became standard in all the decorative establishments in the Stourbridge district. At the time of the coronation of William IV in 1831, glass manufacturers therefore had a wider choice of glassware with which to mark the coronation of the new King.

One of the most progressive manufacturers was Apsley Pellatt,[2] who, at the early age of thirty, owned and operated the Falcon Glassworks in Southwark. He developed a process of forming 'Cameo-Incrustation' in glass, and another in which portraits were impressed in deep intaglio fashion on such articles as scent-bottles. These articles were popular coronation mementoes. One is shown in Plate 14(E), a scent-bottle showing an excellent bust of William IV, with the impressed inscription W.IV.R. Other popular glasses at the time of the coronation of William IV were rummers engraved

[1] See p. 88.   [2] See p. 17.

15. JACOBITE GLASSES

A, B, C: Glasses engraved with oak leaf, the heraldic rose, the star and other emblems of the Jacobite Cause. D, E: Jacobite glasses engraved with the thistle, the Scottish counterpart of the heraldic rose. F: Portrait glass with engraving of Prince Charles Edward, the Young Pretender (*Mr Cecil Davis*).

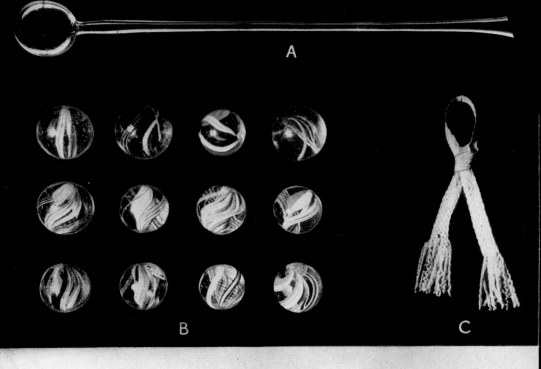

16. MISCELLANEOUS GLASSWARE

A: Yard-of-ale glass (*Victoria and Albert Museum*). B: Glass marbles with coloured twists; late 19th century (*Mr J. W. Edwards*). C: Tie made of strands of finely spun coloured glass. D: Toddy-lifter (*Tolson Memorial Museum, Huddersfield*). E: Jelly-glass with double swan-neck handles; early 18th century (*Mr Cecil Davis*). F: Coloured Vase lustre with prismatic icicle pendants; late 19th century (*Mr John Northwood*).

with such emblems as the vine and grapes with the inscription 'King Wm the 4th'.

The coronation of the monarchs from the time of Victoria to the present Queen have been well recorded in glassware of all descriptions. During this period there has been a marked improvement in style. There has been a definite break from hackneyed patterns of the Victorian era; indeed, most of the glassware for the recent coronation was designed to be in harmony with the present age, while the craftsman himself has a new vitality and creative sense. Traditional forms and styles have not been without their influence, however, but in most cases they have been absorbed and reproduced with a distinct modern touch.

Typical of the glass in this category is a loving cup (Plate 14, F) of which only fifty pieces were made. The cup is inscribed with the Royal coat of arms, Her Majesty's words of dedication of service, and symbols of the Commonwealth countries.

Many types of glassware commemorating the coronation of Her Majesty Queen Elizabeth II made their appearance at the time, mostly engraved with the Royal cipher and date. They included powder-bowls, vases, butter-dishes, ash-trays, cocktail shakers and drinking glasses of all shapes and sizes.

JACOBITE GLASSES

Other important commemorative glasses are those associated with the Jacobite Cause. They are probably the most popular of the engraved glasses, and are eagerly sought by collectors. Jacobite glasses are fairly numerous, and display a variety of emblems, each presenting a problem as to its hidden meaning. The most important emblem is the Jacobite Heraldic Rose with either six, seven or eight petals; but in addition there are the star, the oak-leaf, butterfly, caterpillars and grubs, carnation, daffodil, forget-me-not, honeysuckle, thistle, lily-of-the-valley and sunflower.

An example of Jacobite glasses with the rose emblem is specimen B in Plate 15. The modern theory is that the rose represents the triple crown, that of Britain, France and Ireland, the small or sinister bud, that on the right of the rose, represents the Old Pretender, and the large or dexter bud on the left represents Prince Charles Edward. In Scotland the thistle was the counterpart of the rose, and Scottish Jacobite glasses display this emblem. Examples are shown in Plate 15(D and E).

It will be noted that the three glasses A, B and C in Plate 15 are engraved with an oak-leaf, specimen B showing the emblem on the foot. The oak-leaf is regarded by some as symbolizing Prince Charles as a grown man, and glasses carrying this emblem are usually regarded as post-Culloden, that is, post-1746. The oak-leaf has many associations with the Stuarts. There is the exploit of Charles II in the Boscobel oak after the Battle of Worcester in 1650, and his wearing of the oak-leaf in commemoration of it when he triumphantly entered London on his Restoration ten years later. The anniversary of this day has become known as Oak-Apple Day, and is held to signify the hope of a second Restoration.

The glass in Plate 15(c) has the word *fiat* and a star engraved near the rim. Many Jacobite glasses carry the former inscription, which, according to modern Jacobite theories, means 'May it come to pass' or 'Let it be so'; it constitutes a prayer that the hopes thus emblematically expressed may be fulfilled. The star has always been regarded as having special significance in connection with Prince Charles; indeed, it is held to represent him.

The specimen F in Plate 15 shows an engraved portrait of Prince Charles Edward, the Young Pretender. This glass is typical of a group of Jacobite glasses and others that were attempts at portraiture on glass during the eighteenth century. In some cases the subjects were equestrian figures. They have no special merit when considered as engravings; indeed, most of them are little more than grotesque effigies. The specimen shown is characteristic of the group; it is obviously the hand of a commercial craftsman, and not of an artist-engraver. Nevertheless, as Jacobite relics, glasses of this nature are eagerly sought by collectors.

During the period of Johnson's influence on glass,[1] that is up to 1761, English porcelain was becoming a vogue. The factories of Chelsea, Bow, Derby, Worcester and others were turning out exquisitely painted ware that had an immediate appeal. It is only to be expected, therefore, that attempts would be made by engravers of glass to imitate the figure subjects most successful with porcelain. Landscapes were attempted, but the limited skill of the engraver and his inability to use his technique to suggest the third dimension, caused them for the most part to be dismal failures. Greater success on glass fell to the enamellers, such as Michael Edkins and the Beilbys, who could employ colour.

One group of engraved glasses, however, which can be traced to the competitive influence of porcelain was that in which the figure subjects were birds, a favourite choice on English porcelain, especially Worcester.

[1] See p. 97.

Glass engraving deteriorated in quality but not in quantity towards the close of the eighteenth century. It was then no longer in the hands of specialists such as Jerom Johnson, but had become a common practice in all glass establishments throughout the country. The naturalistic detail of the flowered glasses gave place to conventional designs and geometric patterns which were mere suggestions of the earlier efforts. Much of the charm that had characterized the flowered period of engraving was thus lost.

CHAPTER TEN

Miscellaneous Glassware

FINGER-BOWLS

AMONG the many miscellaneous items of early glassware that can be picked up today are finger-bowls. They can be obtained in both coloured and colourless glass, and also in opaque white, some painted in enamels in *famille-rose*. Although blue finger-bowls are held by many to be a product exclusively of the Bristol glasshouses, glass bowls in various colours such as blue, green, ruby and amethyst were, of course, made at many glasshouses throughout the country; they had always been a 'safe' product for the glass-maker, for they served a variety of purposes; eighteenth-century notices mentioned punchbowls, bowls for goldfish, fruit-bowls, salad-bowls and glass bowls for sugar, butter, mead, and, fitted with rings, for holding candles.

The English glass-maker, however, interested himself in bowls much earlier than the eighteenth century. There is mention in 1585, for example, of a dozen water-glasses which cost Lord Pembroke four shillings. There is some uncertainty among collectors, however, as to what was meant in the sixteenth century by water-glasses. The early use of them was for rinsing the mouth with water after a meal; the later meaning of the term water-glass was what is meant today by finger-bowl, but the process of transition is somewhat obscure. The early forms were tall and cylindrical vessels, resembling to some extent the modern tumbler; others were waisted and on feet, the bowls with threaded borders and patterned in the style described at the time as 'nipt diamond waies'.

The custom of rinsing the mouth after a meal goes back at least to the sixteenth century. Smollett[1] states that he knew of 'no custom more beastly than that of using water-glasses in which polite company spirt, and squirt, and spue the filthy scouring of their gums'. This outspoken comment did not appear to have brought about the improvement intended, for Twiss,[2] a decade later, complained that 'the filthy custom of using water-glasses after meals is as common as in England'.

The custom, however, was changing about this period, for late in

[1] T. Smollett, *Travells*, 1, V, 1766.
[2] Twiss, *Tour in Ireland*, 1776.

the second half of the century the term 'water-glasses' had given place to 'wash-hand' glasses, still later to 'finger-glasses' and finally to 'finger-bowls'. During the period of transition the shape of the water-glass changed from the tumbler form to the more familiar shallow, cup-shaped or straight-sided bowls.

Water-glasses were sometimes provided with a glass cover, known in the eighteenth century as a 'plate'. The earliest reference to them is in *Aris's Birmingham Gazette* of January 23, 1764. The covers were made to match the bowls, and usually terminated in a small knop finial.

Finger-bowls from the second half of the eighteenth century are fairly common, and can be obtained in sets up to half-a-dozen. The usual style is a straight-sided or cup-shaped bowl with double lips, from three and a half to five inches in width and between three and four inches in height. Those in flint are often plain, but some are found decorated with light cutting, such as stars and hollows, flat flutes and splits. Those in opaque white are sometimes painted in coloured enamels in the usual Chinese *famille-rose*.

WINE-GLASS COOLERS

Parallel with the development of the finger-bowl was that of another somewhat similar type of bowl, the wine-glass cooler. Towards the end of the seventeenth century, the idea was introduced of placing a wine-glass in a bowl of cold water in order to cool it for the wine. Wood,[1] the Oxford diarist, records the event in 1683 as follows: 'This year, in the summer time came up a vessel or bason notched at the brims to let drinking glasses hang by the foot, so that the body or drinking place might hang into the water to cool them. Such a bason was called "Monteigh" from a fantastical Scot called Monsieur Monteigh who at that time or a little, wore the bottome of his cloak or coat so notched.'

Dr Johnson in 1773 describes the Montith — his own spelling — as a 'vessel in which glasses are washed'. The monteith was not always in the glass medium however; metal, delft, china and porcelain specimens are known, but whatever the medium, the fundamental idea was the same, that of resting the glass by its stem in the notches in the side of the basin of ice-water so that the glass bowl became cooled. Monteiths measured from nine to fifteen inches in width and were used for cooling up to six glasses.

Individual wine-coolers in glass, however, became the fashion in the late eighteenth century, when it was then customary to provide

[1] A. à Wood, *The Life of Mr. Anthony à Wood*, Oxford, 1730.

a wine-cooler at the table and two glasses for each diner. After the first glass had been emptied, it was placed upside down in the wine-cooler, while the second wine-glass was in use, preparatory to the serving of a different wine.

A typical wine-glass cooler of this period is shown in Plate 7(E). It is in blue glass with a key-fret border in gilt, and is signed 'I. Jacobs, Bristol'. Wine-glass coolers, as will be noted from this example, were provided with either double or single lips in which the stem of the wine-glass rested.

PUNCH-BOWLS AND TODDY-LIFTERS

Punch came into fashion during the last half of the seventeenth century. It was a drink introduced into this country in consequence of Dutch trade with the East Indies.

There is a reference, for example, in John Evelyn's *Diary* on January 16, 1662, of his visit to an East India vessel lying at Black-wall Dock, 'where we had entertainment of several curiosities, Amongst other spirituous drinks, as punch, etc.'

Punch was served hot or cold, and there are, of course, many recipes for its preparation. An excellent one that has come to me from an early eighteenth-century cookery book consists of rum, sack, honey, lemon and cinnamon — there were supposed by tradition to be five basic ingredients. The 'punch-bowl' quickly became an important ritual in the well-ordered household and, indeed, a critical knowledge of the preparation of punch became part of the education of the fashionable gentleman.

In the early days, a large silver bowl, such as a monteith, was called into service, provided with a removable rim scalloped in order to take the glasses. These were placed in the punch-bowl with the stems resting in the escallops, feet uppermost. They were served at the table in this manner, when the glasses would be removed and the punch prepared at the table. A silver lemon-strainer was hung over the side of the bowl, attached to the silver rim — called the coronet — with a flat silver loop.

The bowls used for punch were generally of silver, but china and pottery bowls are known, and a few glass ones occasionally come to light. They are usually of the late seventeenth-century period, but do not interest collectors because, no doubt, of their size. They were often nearly a foot in height by eight or nine inches in width. The early specimens were beautifully made, and decorated with trailed work and pressed patterns. The stems were short and knopped, and the feet domed. Punch-bowls were made later in the eighteenth century with small feet, and decorated by cutting and engraving.

The ladles used for serving the punch were prepared from various materials. Hard wood, such as beech, willow, or metal, or silver coins thinned by hammering and shaped, or whalebone or horn, were some of the more common. The glass-maker had attempted not too successfully to challenge the popularity of these articles by their reproduction in glass. It was not until the turn of the century, however, that he achieved success by striking an entirely new line. This was the so-called toddy-lifter, claimed by many to have been invented in Scotland,[1] but later made in English and Irish glass-houses. There are Irish specimens in the National Museum, Dublin.

A toddy-lifter was something like a miniature decanter in shape, with a body large enough to hold a glassful of liquid. There was a small hole in the base, which enabled the vessel to be used like a pipette. The lifter was dipped into the punch-bowl, so that it filled itself rapidly through the hole in the base. The thumb was then pressed firmly on the top of the lifter, much as is done on the use of a pipette after the suction of the liquid into the vessel. The pressure of the thumb, of course, creates a vacuum and prevents the liquid from escaping.

The punch, thus imprisoned in the lifter, could then be conveyed safely from the punch-bowl to the glass, and released at will by removing the thumb from the top of the lifter. The action is simple and efficient, and there is no doubt that they were extremely popular at the time. They were decorated by cutting, which greatly added to their neatness and pleasing form. Some lifters had a collar round the somewhat long neck, which served a practical purpose in use, in allowing a rest or grip for the fingers whilst the thumb pressure was being applied. The usual size is about six inches. A typical specimen is that shown in Plate 16(D), now at the Tolson Memorial Museum, Huddersfield.

JELLY-GLASSES

A type of glass vessel for the serving of various kinds of confections has been known since the end of the seventeenth century, and from the early eighteenth century has been designated a jelly-glass. In 1678, May[2] gives the advice to 'serve jelly — run into little round glasses four or five in a dish'. It was the custom at the time to serve jelly-glasses, and glasses intended for sweetmeats, on large glass salvers, some of which were up to twenty inches in width. Between

[1] Arnold Fleming, *Scottish and Jacobite Glass*, Glasgow 1938.
[2] Robert May, *The Accomplisht Cook*, 1678, p. 204.

four and eight jelly glasses were arranged round the salver in circular formation with a larger glass as a centre-piece.

Jelly-glasses were advertised throughout the eighteenth century, and appear in a variety of shapes and sizes. The early type was a small, straight-sided bowl, conical in shape, set directly on to a foot, usually with some sort of gadrooning, or a collar containing air-beads at the junction of the bowl to the foot. The foot itself could be plain, folded, or domed and folded. This style persisted until about 1710, when the fashion changed to a bell-shaped bowl also set directly on to a foot, which in this case was usually domed. These glasses were still small — between four and five inches in height — and were attractively decorated, in a variety of ways. Some were provided with a single handle or with a pair, one on either side, in the swan-neck style, which could be plain or alternatively double-looped, that is, the usual swan-neck shape with the bottom curled and elaborated into a definite loop. A typical specimen is that shown in Plate 16(E). The bowls were either plain or were embellished by effective moulded patterns, of which vertical ribs, or pearl or diamond patterns were the most popular.

There is no doubt that the jelly-glasses from this period are excellent examples of the craftsmanship of the early eighteenth-century glass-maker. They were well designed and finely made vessels, shaped and decorated at the furnace mouth by the few simple tools at the command of the glass-maker, and displaying, without the necessity of applied decorative effects, all the inherent beauty and charm of the medium.

These styles persisted up to 1745, the year of the Glass Excise Act, after which the glasses were made lighter and smaller, and such features as handles were dispensed with. The shape of the bowl was retained, but the moulded patterns were replaced by cut motifs. Although an occasional glass is found with hollow diamonds, cut in shallow form, the most popular pattern was vertical fluting, each alternate flute enriched along its edge by a series of continuous hollows. Often the rim of the bowl was scalloped to correspond with the radial flutes, a style which came into fashion about 1760. The feet were sometimes cut with radial flutes.

An occasional glass from this period was with an hexagonal-shaped bowl attached either direct to a foot or with a button or flattened knop. Another style was a straight-sided bowl with slightly flared mouth, which is described by some writers as the 'Hogarth type', because they follow the form of the heavy tavern glasses shown in several of Hogarth's pictures, such as 'The Rake's Progress', the four 'Election Pictures' and 'A Modern Midnight Conversation'.

Jelly-glasses are comparatively common, and because they are not considered as important glasses by the keen collector they can be purchased relatively cheaply. They are often sold in sets of half-a-dozen.

YARDS-OF-ALE

John Evelyn records the following interesting event in his *Diary* on February 10, 1685: 'Being sent to by the Sheriff of the County to appeare, and assist in proclayming the King, I went the next day to Bromely, where I met the Sheriff and the Commander of the Kentish Troop, with an appearance, I suppose, of above 500 horse, and innumerable people, two of his Majesty's trumpets and a Serjeant with other officers, who having drawn up the horse in a large field neere the towne, march'd thence, with swords drawne, to the market-place, where making a ring, after sound of trumpets and silence made, the High Sheriff read the proclaiming titles to his Bailiffe, who repeated them aloud, and then after many shouts of the people, his Majesty's health being drunk in a flint glasse of a yard long, by the Sheriff, Commander, Officers and cheife Gentlemen, they all dispers'd, and I return'd.'

This is the first reference to those yard-long glasses known today as yards-of-ale, of which the capacity is something like one pint. It would appear that in the seventeenth century, when the yard-of-ale glass came in for a certain amount of popularity, it was provided with a foot similar to other styles of glasses. Owing to their extremely fragile nature, yards-of-ale were obviously only used on special occasions, such as that referred to by John Evelyn, and no doubt much care was necessary in using the glass because of its great length.

Modifications of them without feet were employed as trick glasses. These later styles were provided with a bulb at the end, such as that shown in Plate 16(A), which increased the difficulty of using them still further. One who had had no experience of an ale-yard would be presented with a full measure. The unfortunate victim could by exercising great care, overcome the initial stages of emptying the glass until it was tilted finally for the remaining portion. The inrush of air into the now elevated bulb would cause the remainder of the ale to squirt into the face of the drinker as if from the jet of a hose.

The ale-yards vary in length from thirty inches to over a yard. Some have more than one bulb at the end, and in others the usual smooth spherical bulb is slightly fluted or modified to acorn shape. Because of their fragility, few ale-yards have survived the test of time.

GLASS FIBRE

Glass fibre, in spite of its many modern industrial applications, is not a new product. It was made two thousand years ago in Egypt and Rome. There is a specimen[1] in the British Museum of a small glass representation of a human bust and head with a lock of hair hanging over the forehead. The hair is no thicker than a horse hair, yet under magnification, its section is found to consist of nine alternate layers of transparent and opaque glass.

It is impossible to say when glass silk was first made in this country. Animals and exotic flowers, glass ships being tossed on a foaming sea of glass wool, and many other such novelties, have come to us from the last century, and were much in vogue at the time of the Great Exhibition. A glass tie made about this period, woven from fine glass threads, is shown in Plate 16(c). It is made from blue and white strands, composed of threads less than a thousandth of an inch in thickness, of opaque blue and white glass.

The process then used was to spin the glass by heating a glass rod under a flame. A thread was continuously drawn from the soft glass, and wound round a large wooden wheel. By carefully synchronizing the speed of the wheel and the movement of the rod into the flame, it was possible to draw a thread of even thickness until all the rod was used. Many miles of continuous thread were drawn in this manner at a speed of something between fifty and one hundred feet each second. The threads were then treated in much the same manner as cotton or silk and made into novelties such as the glass tie illustrated. Such articles are rare, but are occasionally found in the Stourbridge district and in Lancashire.

GLASS MARBLES

The glass marble no doubt originated from the *margaritai* and *perlai*, the Venetian craftsmen who made glass beads. The art of making beads dates from the early sixteenth century. The process consisted of breaking a glass rod, which had a small hole through its entire length, into short sections. The pieces were then placed, in a mixture of sand and charcoal, in an iron vessel which was rotated and at the same time heated. As the glass slowly softened under the heat, the edges became removed by the rotary motion of the furn-

[1] *The Catalogue of the Slade Collection*, No. 93.

ace, until the beads were completely round. They were then allowed to cool, shaken in bags to remove the stoppings, and finally polished.

Glass marbles were made in much the same manner, with the difference that it was only necessary to use solid glass rod, as the central hole was not required. The rods were made from coloured enamel twists, prepared in the manner described[1] for the making of latticinio or for the making of stems for opaque-twist glasses.[2]

A typical collection of glass marbles is shown in Plate 16(B). They were popular playthings for children about the change of the nineteenth century up to perhaps the beginning of the first World War. The London slang word for them was 'glarnies', which may have been a cockney twist for 'glass alleys', by which name they were known in the North Country. The twists in them were made in a variety of colours both in transparent and opaque glass, and many contained a pleasing blend of different colours.

COLOURED VASE LUSTRES

There is an increasing interest today in the coloured lustres of Victorian days. The usual style is a vase shaped something like a chalice, with scalloped rim, up to a foot in height. Long prismatic lustres, similar to the icicle pendants of the candelabra of the same period, hung from the rim of the bowl in close fringe formation, and gave out a silvery musical note when a gust of wind from an open door or window caused them to collide gently with one another. A typical specimen is shown in Plate 16(F).

These vases were usually in pairs, and were accorded a place of honour on the mantleshelf, one at each end. They were more decorative than functional; they could have contained flowers, but one never saw them used for this or any other purpose.

Coloured lustres came into fashion at the time of the Great Exhibition. Count Harrach, who operated a glassworks at Neuwelt in Bohemia, displayed a group of vases at the Exhibition which excited much comment in the Press. *The Birmingham Journal* of May 31, 1851, suggested 'the purchase of a collection of Bohemian glass which will be accessible to our workmen', and *The Times* of June 7, 1851, stated that 'in glass we cannot equal the ornamental manufactures of Bohemia'.

The Bohemian style favoured colour, and was a reaction against the vogue of crystal glass set by the Stourbridge craftsmen. New colours were produced, such as rich rubies, pale greens from ura-

[1] See p. 54.　　　[2] See p. 86.

nium, blues and amethysts. These were given an opaque white or pale pink overlay, and then cut away in patterns to disclose the coloured under layer. Gilding in which gold leaf was applied with varnish, gave an effective finish to such decoration.

The English glass-makers profited from the advice of the Press. They adopted the Bohemian style of decoration, but reproduced it for home consumption with a strong native flavour. The pendent icicle lustre is typical of Victorian over-emphasis, but it paid handsome dividends at the time. A pair of coloured vase lustres graced every suburban mantleshelf. Despite the fragility of the pendants, many specimens appear to have survived the test of time quite successfully, and are finding their way into collections.

Selected Bibliography

ADAM, R. and J., *The Works in Architecture*. 3 vols. London, 1778–1822.

BERGSTROM, E. H., *Old Glass Paperweights*. London, 1947.

BUCKLEY, F., *History of Old English Glass*. London, 1925. 'Enamel Glass.' *Glass*, vol. viii, pp. 278–280 (1931).

CHARLESTON, R. J., 'Michael Edkins and the Problem of English Enamelled Glass.' *Transactions of the Society of Glass Technology*, vol. xxxviii, pp. 3–16 (1954).

CHURCHILL, ARTHUR AND CO., *History in Glass*. London, 1937. *Glass Notes*.

DILLON, E., *Glass*. London, 1907.

ELVILLE, E. M., 'Glass Paperweights.' *Apollo*, vol. xlvii, pp. 93–94 (1948). 'The History of the Glass Chandelier.' *Country Life Annual*, pp. 200–204 (1949). *English Tableglass*. London, 1951. *English and Irish Cut Glass*, 1750–1950. London, 1953. 'French Paperweights.' *Country Life*, vol. cxiii, pp. 1879–1881 (1953).

FANE, Sir S. PONSONBY, 'Club Pole Heads in Somerset.' *Connoisseur*, vol. xvii, pp. 256–262 (1907).

FLEMING, A., *Scottish and Jacobite Glass*. Glasgow, 1938.

FRANCIS, G. R., *Old English Drinking Glasses*. London, 1926.

GRAY, H. ST G., 'Nailsea Glass.' *Connoisseur*, vol. xxx, pp. 85–98 (1911).

HAYNES, E. B., *Glass Through the Ages*. London, 1948.

HONEY, W. B., *Glass*. London, 1946.

HORRIDGE, W., 'The Rose and Emblems on Jacobite Drinking Glasses.' *Transactions of the Circle of Glass Collectors*, No. 56.

IMBERT, R. and AMIC, Y., *Les Presse-Papiers Français*. France, 1948.

PELLATT, A., *Glass Manufactures*. London, 1821. *Curiosities of Glassmaking*. London, 1849.

ROBERTSON, R. A., *Chats on Old Glass*. London, 1954.

THORPE, W. A., *A History of English and Irish Glass*. 2 vols. London, 1929. *English Glass*. London, 1935.

WAY, W. H. L., 'Glass Paperweights.' *Connoisseur*, vol. lviii (1920).

WESTROPP, M. S. D., *Irish Glass*. London, 1920.

WHISTLER, LAURENCE, *The Engraved Glass of Laurence Whistler*. London, 1952.

Index

114